FINDING ME
~ in ~
# France

Bobbi French

St. John's, Newfoundland and Labrador
2012

We gratefully acknowledge the financial support of the Canada Council for the
Arts, the Government of Canada through the Canada Book Fund (CBF),
and the Government of Newfoundland and Labrador through the Department of
Tourism, Culture and Recreation for our publishing program.

Cover design and layout by Neil McCulloch
Photography by Neil McCulloch and Bobbi French
Printed on acid-free paper

Published by
CREATIVE PUBLISHERS
an imprint of CREATIVE BOOK PUBLISHING
a Transcontinental Inc. associated company
P.O. Box 8660, Stn. A
St. John's, Newfoundland and Labrador A1B 3T7

Printed in Canada by:
TRANSCONTINENTAL INC.

Library and Archives Canada Cataloguing in Publication

French, Bobbi, 1968-
    Finding me in France / Bobbi French.

ISBN 978-1-897174-94-4

1. French, Bobbi, 1968-. 2. Semur-en-Auxois (France)-- Biography. I. Title.

DC801.S4437F74 2012   944'.42   C2012-901094-4

To the Kids

~ Contents ~

~ ONE LIFE ENDS ~

GRACE

I was raised by a Newfoundland family who cherish their deeply held traditions of guilt, panic and self-loathing, so becoming a psychiatrist was the path of least resistance. That way I could put an end to my mother's obsessive fear that I would somehow wind up depending on a man for money. I could also begin the futile quest for the approval of my physician father. But the best part was I could prove to myself (and everyone else) that I wasn't a total idiot. It was the perfect plan. Who wouldn't want a life chosen by a high school kid? Never mind that I had dreams of becoming an improvisational comedic performer discovered by Lorne Michaels who happened to drop in to see my senior year play. As my mother wisely reminded me, I would always be poor if I had to rely on my talent, so medical school it was.

Some 20 years later I was standing in the darkness of my state of the art kitchen at four o'clock on a cold February morning. Insomnia and I had become old friends. On that particular morning it wasn't the usual myriad of stresses and heartbreaks of my life as a child and adolescent psychiatrist that kept sleep at bay. No, this was something new; some sort of fundamental problem, a restlessness taking root in my being. Maybe I was just tired or old. I certainly had a right to be either. The latter by virtue of my 42 birthdays, the former by way of a career that had bled me dry. So I did what any psychiatrist would do, I reflected on myself until my brain hurt.

I don't recall the moment when I knew for sure that I was completely ordinary. I was surprised to realize it. This insight developed slowly and subtly in my consciousness guided by the steady stream of extraordinary kids in the chair across from me. They'd slouch and face me, looking for wisdom or answers or pills or for me to absorb their rage and angst. And no matter how unfortunate or ill or disorganized, they were always impressively uncommon; battered, suicidal, hysterical, psychotic, sexual sophisticates navigating their way often without a moment of love in their lives. Yet there they were, self-aware, confident albeit superficially, clear in purpose even if it was to cause as much self-destruction as possible.

I imagined myself at 16, sure, free of razor cuts on my arms and suicidal depression but also free of confidence, independence and courage. They read Thoreau and strutted their stuff on YouTube. Cripes, I was reading *Anne of Green Gables* and wearing three layers of clothes to pretend that I wasn't six feet tall and 118 pounds (freak not chic). I behaved myself, did well at school, clung to a boyfriend who treated me badly and played the Good Catholic, well, apart from being on the pill. At first I assumed it was generational, that had I grown up texting and blogging and shopping at H & M I would have been their equal, slick as could be, Brazilian wax and all. But in my heart I knew it was a lie. I knew that not once had I ever done anything brave or unexpected.

I love these kids. I love that they prevail despite all odds. I love that they dare to see beyond their despair. They know that no matter what they decide disapproval will ensue and they do it anyway. Not for a moment do I envy their illnesses and suffering or how society hasn't offered them a place at the table for sick kids who deserve compassion and funding. I do, however, respect their predicament and their grace and dignity in tolerating it. They are fundamentally special. I was the one without grace and I needed to find it somewhere.

There were two other things of which I was certain. I love my husband. I look at him and see the only right path I have ever taken. And, something had to give. My career so heavy with serious responsibility didn't fit me anymore. The system had beaten me down. Some days I felt it was killing me, like some sort of disease destroying me body and soul, and that's no way to live. So what was an ordinary gal to do?

Now maybe a four a.m., carbohydrate fuelled, middle-aged malaise wasn't the optimal moment for major life decisions. And it could've just been the chips and chocolate talking, but as I looked at the beautiful house that we'd spent a year renovating, my luxury SUV in the driveway and my action packed calendar that paid for all the things in my gaze, I realized for the first time in my life that I had a choice. I didn't have to wait for the stars and moon to align or until I had a pile of money saved. I didn't have to wait for the elusive perfect job for wayward psychiatrists to miraculously present itself to me. I could simply walk away. My contract at the hospital was up for renewal and I had a decision to make. I could either go ahead and make my deal with the devil like I'd done every year for the past fifteen or I could do something different, something completely illogical.

So I made a deal with myself to abandon the path that I'd travelled for so long. To hell with ordinary, convention, fear of disappointing others, seeking approval and doing what's expected of me. I decided to follow in the footsteps of the great George Costanza and live in the opposite. To be brave and do things I have only dreamed of doing, to turn my life upside down, shake it well and see what comes out. The only thing left was to wake up my better two-thirds and give him the good news. Somehow I knew he'd be in.

And now, three months after that fateful morning, I've done the unthinkable. I resigned from my stable and successful position at a major Canadian hospital, leaving behind an amazing group of people and an equally amazing paycheque. I sold my beautiful house, my car and almost everything I own except for a few essentials, my husband being a perfect example. I purchased a one-way ticket to France, and rented a cottage in Burgundy for a year. I traded stability for the absolute unknown. I have lost my mind. I'm going to look for it in France.

The Joy I've Already Found

But let me back up a bit. Nothing's that simple. While there's no doubt that I'm on some flaky new age (okay middle-age) pilgrimage to joy here, I don't want to give the impression that I existed in some vacuum of doom and gloom. Far from it because I've been blessed beyond measure.

In my life I've been offered many gifts. I grew up on a rock in the North Atlantic in a beautiful culture rich with humour and music, with a language all our own and a fierce determination to survive. My family, flawed though it may be, has made me who I am. I have irreplaceable friends, the kind you would call if you woke up on a cold prison floor in Thailand and they'd know just what to do. I've learned from the best in my career, unbelievably talented and passionate professionals who have devoted their lives to helping teenagers in crisis. I can eat whatever I want and maintain my status as a giant stick insect. I have the best mother-in-law any woman could ever hope for. But by far the greatest gift in my life is my husband Neil, who is without a doubt, joy personified. The world is full of women complaining about their men, and to be sure there's a lot of material to draw from, but I want to be sentimental for a moment in case I ever forget his place in all this.

Everyone who meets Neil is better for it. I've never seen anything like it. People spend five minutes with him during which he may say five words and they walk away thinking how wonderful he is. It's like he has his own atmosphere with a gravitational pull. I think back on how "I" became "we" and I shudder at how easily I could have missed it. One different decision, one small misstep in time and I would have passed him by.

It seems I have a habit of marrying fine men. My first walk down the aisle was at the ripe old age of 23. He was lovely, I grew up and we grew apart. We're both happy now, end of story. After my first marriage ended, I moved to Ontario to learn how to work with teenagers. I stayed longer than I thought I would, longer than I should have. And while it wasn't all bad, after almost five years on the mainland (as we Newfoundlanders like to say), I knew I needed a change of scene. I decided to head back east and found myself a job in Halifax, Nova Scotia. Even then I had dreams of Europe but I thought I needed to focus on my career.

So, as usual, I worked and worked some more. I made some new friends but as for dating, well, I discovered that after ten years away from the game my reflexes were off and all the rules had changed. I couldn't tell the good from the bad from the ugly. I couldn't even get a condom out of the package let alone figure out how to use one. The hair removal ritual alone was enough to make me want to pack it in. If I could've gone on dates with furry legs and bushy armpits I would've been far more into it. Finally, after a lovely evening of being grilled over dinner about my suit-ability as a DNA provider, I decided I would have no more of this madness and hung up my razor. The only thing I would commit to was befriending a man who would accompany me to fancy balls (I'd never been to one in my life but you never know) and take care of any heavy lifting. I wasn't discouraged or defeated; I just really liked being on my own. I did, however, remain open to meeting an aging millionaire who, now weary with supermodels, was seeking a companion to share expensive dinners, someone with whom he could have long chats about feminism while redecorating his many homes around the globe.

Birthday number 34 rolled around and my dear friend Judy (mother of three small boys, so more to be pitied than blamed) wanted a grownup Friday night out. We started at an upscale bar packed to the rafters with people who all seemed to be desperately searching for something. After an excruciating hour enduring a man's obviously well rehearsed I'm-a-fancy-pants-doctor routine (he didn't once ask me what I did), I hit the jackpot with a charming and married musician from my hometown. We chatted for ages about music, the old country, and life in general. Now this was a perfect evening for me—libations with a beloved friend and an interesting man to chat with who had no designs on clubbing me over the head and dragging me home.

Then Judy, empowered by three drinks and her freedom from diapers, exclaimed, "Let's go dancing!" Yes, I thought, let's abandon this perfectly delightful setup and go scream at each other while half-naked college girls perform choreographed dance numbers and their boyfriends crush beer cans on their heads. But who am I to keep a good mother down? So, whining and complaining all the way, I allowed myself to be dragged to the Velvet Olive, a local pose and pick-up joint. It's a good thing nobody ever listens to me. Had I known what was inside waiting for me I would have broken down the door.

The club was of the standard meat market variety; a blue-lit bar, a bald, tattooed waitress and firm-bodied young-and-eligibles fully engaged in age-old mating rituals. Clearly more drinks were necessary for this mess so we queued up for the privilege of paying 13 bucks for a martini. I was squished into a man wearing painter-pant jeans and a T-shirt with holes around the neck. He looked mostly blue from the glow of the bar as he put out his hand, "Hi, I'm Neil." We got to shouting in each other's ear about his work in advertising, that he spoke Spanish, how I was there with friends for my birthday. At one point he smiled widely and Judy and I both stepped back from the blinding glare of the strobe light bouncing off his face full of teeth. He'd seen this reaction before and like a proud third grader he beamed, "And I never had braces!" We'd stumbled upon the last truly beguiling man on the planet.

Then, quite out of the blue (literally), he slapped his hand down on the bar as if to seal a deal. "So, I want to see you again. What are you doing tomorrow?" I just blinked at him. He was happy with drink but by no means drunk. He surely could've won the affections of any of the fresh-faced, recently shaved gals in the place, so I was confused. I broke out my patented slick dating banter: "I'm sort of dating someone, well not dating really, okay a couple of dates but I have to end it because he's really quite wrong for me and I'm likely going to be staying single now plus I don't know if you noticed but I am a bit taller than you. Also I'm a psychiatrist, which everyone hates, you know, on account of their fear of being analyzed, so …" What the hell was wrong with me? He didn't even flinch: "One, I always date tall women, and B, the last woman I dated was a resident in psychiatry. So, about tomorrow?" I was totally flustered by this time. "Well, my friend Judy is visiting for the weekend so I can't…" Before I could finish, he was at it again, "When is she leaving? I have these theatre tickets for Sunday night so you can come with me. No problem." So, quite unromantically, because I didn't know what to do with him, I handed him my business card. And that was that.

Monday morning, I arrived at the hospital yet another year older but not one bit wiser and there it was, the small rectangle of pink paper that read "8:59 a.m. — Please call Neil." I held it in my hand and sighed. No, I would not be distracted or pulled off track. I called to tell him so but there was no denying how excited he was to hear from me. Right. Well, I thought, I suppose it would be rude to brush him off on the phone. Instead, I agreed to have a coffee with him that evening before meeting up with some friends. I'd tell him that he was a charming man but I'd resolved to be single. How hard could it be?

I put no effort into preparing to meet this Neil fellow because it wasn't really a date; it was a coffee to say it wasn't a date. I remember exactly what I wore: a faded blue T-shirt with only half the hem intact, jeans that hadn't actually made contact with my arse in some time, scuffed loafers and a ratty, pilled sweater coat. I can't recall whether I bothered with lipstick or not but I do know that I didn't so much as brush my hair. When I got to the coffee shop I saw him sitting quietly reading a paper and looking sharp in his crisp shirt and new jeans. He was perched under a halogen light, his orange hair was like fire and his skin was the palest hue of rosy peach. He was completely iridescent and absolutely beautiful. Where the hell was the blue guy with the torn shirt, the frat boy who'd forgotten he graduated? As I looked at him, I felt a familiar flush of humiliation from head to toe, high school all over again. But then again maybe this would be easier than I thought. He'd take one look at me, run out the door screaming and leave me to my beloved freedom.

Instead, we sat and talked. Fifteen minutes later, I knew that he was warm and witty and entirely engaging. By the time I'd finished my second cup of tea, I knew that he was an open and honest man who was clever and confident without a hint of arrogance. And by the end of the evening, I knew that he was the happiest person I'd ever met. I felt happy just being near him. He walked me to my car and I was disappointed to see him go. I was oddly compelled to email him the next day to thank him and to say that I kind of wished we'd had more time together. He emailed back, charm firing on all cylinders, and we agreed to go for dinner. We ate and talked until we were the only people left in the restaurant. Everything became clear and quiet and time seemed to stop. He reached across the table for my hand and I knew it was over, my solitary life, all my plans to be wild and free. I knew that I had to keep him, that he would be good for me in every way. For once in my life I stopped thinking and just let things be.

Eight months into it we each sold our houses, bought one together and started tearing it up. Three houses later on a sunny day in the Boboli Gardens in Florence he reached into his fanny pack and unwrapped a diamond ring from a tissue (no one's perfect), which led to a wedding in a hair salon/café/art gallery officiated by a Buddhist couple from Brooklyn. Of course we've had our share of relationship challenges (me), but I know whatever happens in my life, he will always be the best decision I ever made. You know what they say, if you want to make god laugh, tell her your plans. I've learned to make fewer plans, keep an open mind and graciously accept whatever she offers me.

Neil is my touchstone and greatest ally. Who else would respond to my, "I think we should abandon my big income, sell everything we own, have you drag your work overseas so I can find myself," with a simple, "Sounds good, my love"? He makes me a gourmet dinner every night; he's kindhearted and goofy and ridiculously intelligent. He speaks three languages, cries at movies, dances with abandon and loves his family. He's everything from photographer to handyman and generates an energy that's hard to describe. People are drawn to him like moths to the flame; maybe it's his flaming red hair that beckons. He's out of my league and I know it. It can't be easy to live with a gigantic, feminist psychiatrist.

So I thank whatever is up there for every moment I have spent with him and I thank him for his peaceful soul. I'll be hanging on to him like he was the last teak lounger on the Lido deck of the Titanic. It is a miracle that he loves me, it is a miracle that he puts up with me. Maybe it's a miracle when anybody loves anyone. What I do know is that my miracle has been loving him. Now if only I could train him to use the laundry hamper.

FRANCE? POURQUOI?

As we prepare to leave, everyone I run into these days asks the same thing, why France? And it's a good question. It's not like we spun a globe, closed our eyes and pointed. Maybe it is somewhat impulsive to run away from your life, but it wasn't all madness without method.

When I first met Neil I was so impressed by his travels. He'd been on a safari tour in Africa; I'd been to a zoo in Toronto. He did his last year of high school in the south of France; I once went to a Canadiens game in Montreal. He lived for a year in Spain; I ate Mexican food at Zapata's on Bates Hill in St. John's. He drove across America in a beater truck with his buddy Steve; I once drove three hours from St. John's to Marystown in fog so thick you could lean on it. My single major travel experience had been a trip to England with my grandmother when I was 16. From that moment on I knew I wanted to see Europe but somehow my life was always in the way.

When Neil and I first went to Italy in 2007, I was completely undone by it all—the cuisine, the history and the pace of life. But for me it was something deeper than museums and cathedrals. I knew that I belonged in Europe. I was convinced that I had been living someone else's life and that every woman I saw in Europe was living mine. I knew I needed to return as soon as I could. We came home, took Italian lessons, bought Italian cookbooks and fantasized constantly about living *la dolce vita* someday.

We were planning our third Italian vacation when, while watching a movie set in the French town where Neil went to school, he said, "You know, I'd like to go back to France." Holy mackerel man, pick a language. I already knew how to order a lot of food in Italian, plus I had most of the vulgar hand gestures just right. But I wasn't about to turn down the chance to see another European country. I dusted off the very little French I knew and we began our yearly quest for discounted plane tickets.

I loved France as much as I loved Italy. For me, Rome was passion and pandemonium while Paris was restrained sophistication. The rural areas were breathtaking as expected. And as we had done in Italy, we rented a small village house and spent four weeks living as locals. Like always, we came home to our busy lives and had dreamy bedtime chats about a new life in Europe that ended with wistful sighs and an alarm clock set for the next day.

After our first vacation in France I was finally inspired enough to wade through the paperwork required for my UK passport, a privilege granted by my dad's birth in Surrey, which also conveniently makes me an EU citizen. The day it arrived I was positively euphoric. I nearly drove Neil to distraction as I spent an entire weekend pretending I was Jason Bourne. It was then that the idea of moving really started cooking. With the passport I could live anywhere in the European Union and drag my poor one passport spouse with me.

Suddenly, the fantasy of a life in Europe took on a tinge of reality and we began talking more and more about where we would settle someday when we finally won the lottery. We knew that we wouldn't want to live anywhere we hadn't actually seen and the tickets for a second trip to France were booked. Neil already spoke French quite well and there were other practical considerations like France's highly regarded health care system. Italy had always been the focus of our dreams, but I'd decided I couldn't live there as long as Berlusconi was running the show. The man actually said, "Mussolini never killed anyone, he just sent dissenters abroad for vacation." The same man who also advised investment in Italy because "we have beautiful secretaries, really superb girls," but I digress. So we decided to use our vacation in Burgundy as a recon mission (a term I learned in the espionage training reserved for people with more than one passport) for a move someday far off in the future when everything was right.

So there we were in the small medieval town of Semur-en-Auxois, about 270 kilometers southeast of Paris, chosen solely based on a pretty vacation house I'd unearthed after countless hours of searching online. The sun was shining, the town was charming and the locals welcoming. For three days it was perfect. Then the skies grew dark, the rain fell and the temperature plummeted to ten degrees and stayed there for two weeks. When the sun finally made a brief reappearance I raced to the terrace with my book and a big glass of wine. I had just settled for a little *vie en rose* when a young woman ambled down the drive. She was an English woman who managed a vacation property in the town. We'd had some email exchanges with her a few months before and she was dropping by just to say hello. We got to chatting about the many renovations we'd done in Canada, our interest in property and our dream of someday living in Europe. I noticed a peculiar expression on her face while we were talking, like she was clicking through something in her mind, but I thought nothing of it at the time. We shared the wine and said our goodbyes.

Over the next two weeks we had one problem after another. The cold, wet weather continued. Every day I wore the same ugly sweater I'd thankfully brought as an afterthought to protect my computer. The septic tank at the house failed creating a pervasive sewer-like odour that was starting to seep into our skin. The bed was like a rock. Every morning, a symphony of critters in the attic performed steadily from two a.m. until dawn. When the roof started leaking and we became overrun with ants, we thought all this mess was a sign that maybe Semur didn't suit us. Now having been immersed in science for most of my life, signs and fate and all that have never been big for me. But every now and then you have to stop and pay attention, just slow down and listen.

In the midst of things going from bad to worse, we got a call from the lovely English woman who said she and her business associate would like to get together to chat about what they do in France. As it turned out, their vacation property management business was overrun with clients and they'd been planning to launch a search for a couple to help expand their business. They pitched it to us as they felt we were just the people they were looking for and that they couldn't imagine a better fit for them. We would start by maintaining and marketing vacation houses in our area then gradually move into conducting property searches and full-scale renovations for Francophiles with money to burn. They were even looking for someone to help with branding and marketing, which happens to be Neil's area of expertise. Hmm. What were the odds? Neil's work was relatively portable with a manageable level of difficulty. We had no kids to consider. I was smack in the middle of some sort of mid-life burnout mayhem. Plus, I had the passport. It felt like all the stars were aligning to show the path to a new life.

Of course, because I wanted this so badly, I started thinking about all the reasons not to do it. I don't have enough money saved. We just bought a house we love and it's in the middle of a full-scale renovation. I don't speak French very well, the understatement of the year. I don't like escargot or really smelly cheese. I don't have what it takes to start over at 42. Neil will run away with an exotic French woman, leaving me homeless in the cobblestone streets of France. Once it got this ridiculous, I moved into what-the-hell mode. When will I ever get a chance like this again? We'll go. If it's horrible, we'll come back and start over. I had no other employment options other than to do the same thing I'd been doing, just in a different place. Not appealing. Sure, we'd have no house and no possessions if it went belly-up but what else was there to lose?

So, after more discussion with the Brits and some significant soul searching in my kitchen, I made the commitment to give it all up and return in the fall to see what was waiting for me in this strange place. The very long answer to the question is while all roads lead to Rome, all signs point to France.

A LIFE FOR SALE,
GOING CHEAP

Now that the decision to leave has been definitively made, the process has taken on a life of its own. My glorious *bon voyage* dinners and parties have come and gone and I've said my teary goodbyes to a dream team I helped build. Leaving my work was a remarkably bittersweet affair and I guess letting go of anything so substantial always is. It seems letting go has become a new mantra of mine and it applies not only to my career but to my possessions as well. I envision it as a peaceful detachment, a state I will achieve when I overcome my desire for worldly things and thus attain a heightened and enlightened perspective. Ah, how Zen of me, how remarkably serene. Not really. The truth of it is the little French cottage we've rented cannot hold all our worldly things and the bother and cost of storing or shipping everything is just not practical. My shrink senses tell me that a clean break is in order here, not to mention the much-needed cash that a middle-age meltdown sale will generate. So, over the last couple of weeks we've been tossing and tagging all the things that made up our life.

As a friend of mine was browsing around our living room, she asked if I was struggling with relinquishing anything, and it got me to thinking. My first thought was how can two people possibly have so much stuff? We have three televisions, two cars, dishes we never use, furniture we only look at and a garage full of every tool imaginable including a power-washer thing that could take the paint off a ship. My second thought was to wonder to what extent my life was defined by my things and whether I was truly at peace with pulling away.

I've never been very sentimental when it comes to material things, but as I looked around my house I was surprised to find a memory attached to just about everything. I looked at my Danish mid-century modern teak dining set and remembered the months and months of obsessively combing the Internet until I found it on eBay about three o'clock one winter morning. I had it shipped right across Canada and not a day went by that I didn't admire its beauty. But it costs more to ship it than I paid for it and I have to let it go. It's off to my friend's stylish condo and she will sit and eat dinner with her daughters and sip wine with her friends and I know she'll love it. Then I unearthed all the Christmas ornaments I spent years accumulating. I sat there holding each one, desperately trying to decide if they were worth the effort. In the end, ruthless purging prevailed and I let them go as well. It was surprisingly comforting to know that so many of our things will be in the homes of people we love.

After our friends finished looting our home we still had half a houseful of stuff, so we listed everything on a local buy-and-sell website. By eight a.m. the next day we had a dozen responses from the same person who finally put it together that all the items were at one house. A couple of hours later I watched from the window as a woman, for whom the word fabulous was clearly invented, arrived in a taxi. She raced up the steps and burst through the door, larger than life, a tornado of hair and heels and rock star attire. She clicked around the house saying, "I'll take that and that and this, ooh and that, how much for this?" In the space of 15 minutes she'd bought everything we had, gave us $1000 in cash as a deposit and dashed out to the waiting cab. It was unlike anything I'd ever seen. We stood in the porch gaping at each other, wondering what the hell had just happened. I later learned that this dynamo was emerging from a very dark and difficult period in her life. She too was making a fresh start and was incredibly grateful to have our things define her new life.

Now we own clothing, a mattress, a few pieces of art, some miscellaneous kitchen items, cameras and our computers. It's an incredible experience to relinquish all the things you own. I didn't quite know how I would feel but I think I feel lighter, free to move about the world at a moment's notice, a nomad of the planet, able to leap tall buildings in a single bound. Is coming unglued the same as being detached?

LIVING IN A
FOREIGN LANGUAGE

Whenever I tell someone about the impending exodus, after the bewildered facial expression fades, they invariably ask, "Do you speak French?" "Oh enough to get by," I say. Sure, enough to order a bottle of 2007 Meursault and a sautéed duck breast although not enough to know that I once ordered the thymus glands of a calf. Of all the things to be concerned with, and there are many, this is the one on my mind at all times. I imagine myself at a party standing alone in a corner, mute and forlorn or, more importantly, unable to communicate in an emergency. Scary.

I'm particularly concerned about this because there are few things in life that I love more than language. I remember reading the same books over and over when I was a kid, thinking it was the best entertainment ever designed. I'm still a ferocious reader, consuming books in a single sitting and staying up all night just to see how an author has woven phrases into a tale. I love words. Jokes, puns, double entendres, the lot. And as for chatting, I could be world champion as soon as my mother retires.

Now the teachings of Buddhism say not to speak unless it improves on silence but anyone who knows anyone in my family can attest to the fact that we feel non-stop yakkety-yak improves any situation. What can I say? It's cultural. I'm Canadian but I don't speak fluent French, the shame of it all. But I'm a Newfoundlander first, and on the Rock, language is sacred. We have an ancient dialect that is formally studied and researched. We're the Latins of Canada. We speak with passion and drama and there is much expression and gesturing, yet we have an economy of language that is unmatched. Also, if you can't weave a good yarn (translation: tell an entertaining story) you get voted off the island and have to move to Alberta. We are famous for our ranting and roaring (well, Rick Mercer is famous for it), for our phrases and colloquialisms, and it's the thing I miss most about my home.

I abandoned French in Grade 9 because my teacher was less than likeable and besides I was never going to work for Air Canada, so why bother? I've resisted it over the years for different reasons. I was too busy for starters and perhaps too politically opposed to the whole "Quebec is the only distinct culture in Canada" nonsense. Here's distinct: try understanding a fisherman from the Burin Peninsula sometime. I certainly can't. But mostly I didn't learn French because I just didn't need to, nor did I have any desire to. After studying Spanish in university, a language that sounds like music to me, French sounded contrived and haughty, like, "I will stoop to speak with you but only because I must." I can roll a Spanish R like Antonio Banderas but I never seem to manage that French back-of-the throat R without hacking up something that I fear will land on someone's face.

But now I have no choice. There is very little English spoken in rural France so off to class I go, three hours every Thursday morning until we leave, then on to lessons with a lovely woman in Semur who has agreed to take me on. I hope she can translate "oh me nerves missus, you got me drove."

FRENCH FOR DUMMIES

I wonder if it's too late to call this whole thing off because I'm not sure I can go on with this madness. I've just finished my first French class with not an English word spoken for three hours. The good news is that I'm second in my class in terms of skill and finesse. The bad news is that there are only two people in my class: a sweet 15-year-old boy preparing to spend a school year abroad, and me.

Based on an online test and a brief personal interview, I was placed at level six of a potential 16 levels. When I first learned this I thought, of course I'm at level six. I've been to France twice, I once successfully purchased cough medicine in France, my hairstylist is French, I've eaten thymus—I'm practically fluent. Not so. It turns out the problem is not that I can't speak French. No, the problem is I can't speak bloody English. The teacher and the boy were identifying predicates and conjunctive adverbs all over the place. Apparently the key to learning a second language is having a firm grasp of your first. If only I hadn't spent Grade 9 English classes memorizing the lyrics for the entire *Rebel Yell* album. I couldn't keep myself focused. The very sweet teacher with her perfect Parisian accent asked me some question about something and the only thought in my head was I wonder if there are any muffins left at the bakery downstairs, followed swiftly by am I too old to wear shorts?

I suppose I have to give myself a break. It's been a long time since I've been in a classroom learning something completely new. But it's also been a long time since I've felt completely useless at something, apart from cooking and math. You work at the same thing for a long time and you get really comfortable in the knowledge that you know what you're doing. The key is to not panic. I can do this. Clearly the 15-year-old can do it.

But French is famously difficult and often seems illogical to me. The French words for vagina, uterus, ovary and feminism are actually masculine and the literal translation for the number 91 is four twenty eleven. I'm convinced people are locked away in castle towers all over the French countryside charged with nothing but the task of inventing new verb tenses. This might be harder than I thought. All I can hope for is when she asks me a question next week I don't respond with, "*Oui Mademoiselle*, ash blonde highlights, think I can pull it off?"

MIND: GONE
JOURNEY: ON

Two months to go and on this very ordinary day I've officially passed the point of no return. Today I inactivated my medical licence and malpractice insurance. Now I've never been one to be attached to titles and hierarchy, all that "call me doctor" nonsense, but let's face it, there is a weird prestige connected to the MD or PhD. Certainly I can imagine the pride my mother will feel knowing her daughter used to be a doctor but now cleans toilets in vacation houses in France. And there is that whole income thing. I weighed the options and considered keeping my licence as a backup plan, but the costs of maintaining everything are enormous. Just to be clear, there's no pile of cash to finance my folly and I have to trim anywhere I can.

I made all the calls and I listened carefully to the warnings from colleagues and the people at the licencing boards, but I don't think they got it. Apparently people don't abandon their medical careers very often. They listened politely but I could tell they were on the other end of the phone twirling their index fingers by their temples while mouthing to their co-workers, "This one is completely gone." But I stood firm, safe in the knowledge that I'd become unhinged long before they found out about it. I wrote up the official emails and hit send. I was instantly overcome by my own courage and sense of purpose. I was bathed in the glow of a new and extraordinary me. This was immediately followed by being bathed in sweat.

UNSEND! UNSEND! What have I done? A full-on wave of anxiety washed over me. For the first time in my life I am unemployed, my last pay comes next week and half a paycheque at that, and now I'm not a doctor any more. Neil found me standing in the kitchen, soaked and shaky, paralyzed with panic. I turned, a column of horror, and told him what I'd done. "Hey, high five," he said, raising his hand in the air for the congratulatory slap, "What's for lunch?"

I love this man. As usual, his calm tempered my storm, the seas parted and rational thought resumed. I wondered if I'd ever really stop being a doctor? On the up side I won't have to deal with my significant fear of being on an airplane and hearing the announcement, "Is there a doctor on the plane?" Every time I fly I think of those doctors who saved a passenger's life using a bag of pretzels and paper clips or some other MacGyver-inspired contraption and I wonder what I'd do in the same situation. At best I could ask them about their invalidating childhood and explore their feelings about dying on an Air Canada flight from Halifax to Montreal.

It's hard to describe the experience of healing. Like anything else, after a while it becomes routine. You deal with the same crisis so many times that knowing what to do often takes no effort. Mostly it's very serious and dark with rays of light here and there. The kids I worked with have stories so heavy that it's hard to imagine how they will ever recover, and yet they do.

Not long ago I received a long, heartfelt letter of gratitude from a mother whose son I cared for while he was seriously ill. Much to everyone's relief he recovered in hospital. She wrote that he was now thriving in school and in life. She thanked me for my compassion and said she was forever grateful to me for saving her son. It was so moving this letter that I was tearful reading it. I was amused, however, when she said she was sure that I received letters like this all the time. Almost never. But that's not the point of doing it. I did it because I took an oath; it was my duty and my job. But make no mistake, it was also my profound privilege and it will be hard to top in terms of its place in the grand scheme of things. Anyway, this whole journey is supposed to be about embracing change and letting go, right? Too bad it doesn't come with benefits and vacation pay.

THE GIFT OF PAIN

Normally I prefer to disclose sordid personal details, particularly health related ones, only to those within my comfort zone. But because I'm living in the opposite these days, I'm supposed to be doing things that challenge me and trust me, this one is tough for me to put out there. So here goes.

Since 1994 I have not lived a day without pain. To make a very long story short I've had three major spinal surgeries, two on my back and more recently one on my neck. No violent car crashes or anything remotely tragic, just faulty discs, the cards I've been dealt. Each episode was fairly dramatic, especially the one with my neck, as my spinal cord was badly compressed and an emergency surgery was necessary to avoid paralysis. For months I'd known that I had a herniated disc in my neck but I ignored the sound medical advice I'd been given (as many doctors do) and kept right on working. Three days before the surgery I remember waking up in the middle of the night with both arms dangling like useless flippers, panicked out of my mind yet hoping the situation would improve by morning so I could get through my day on call. By nine a.m. I had recovered enough to function (barely) and in between assessments in the ER, I begged a radiologist to squeeze me into the MRI machine. We both stood there looking at my films knowing too well the gravity of the situation, him asking why the hell I wasn't seeking care immediately and me offering a smile and a cursory thank you for his time. I raced back to the ER to finish my shift before heading off to another hospital to have my own emergency looked after. I was despondent and terrified, yet my major concern was how the situation would affect my work schedule. This was how I lived. By the way I do not recommend anyone try this at home. Please remember I am a professional fool. Not surprisingly, as soon as I recovered, I began contemplating major changes to my life.

Five years before, my second back surgery had gone horribly wrong leaving me with a paralyzed right leg. At the time I was told that it might recover, it might not, I'd have to wait and see. I'm not big on waiting and seeing so, with the help of some physician colleagues, I organized a rehab program for myself, and after a year of gruelling training, I learned to walk again. I still have major problems with the leg but I can walk, top speed, like I always have. Looking back on it, I have no idea where I found the strength.

This long cycle of damage and repair has left me with scars, titanium plates and screws (but alas no Bionic Woman functions) and a whole lot of chronic pain. I've seen all kinds of doctors and tried all kinds of medications. I've had too many MRIs to count and it has become a very large part of my life. It also played a large role in the decision to move to France, land of the supposedly outstanding health care system. Like everyone, I have good days and bad days. I have a special mattress and pillow. I have to wear very practical shoes, and those stylish purses the size of suitcases? Forget about it. I used to have pretty decent legs and now, let's just say shorts are for heat-wave emergencies only.

It's so easy to focus on the things I can't do. I miss moving without thought or planning, dancing however I want to, just moving through the world without fear of the next disaster. I look at people running and I wonder if they realize their good fortune. I long to be comfortable … oh someone pass the Brie to go with this whine. The reality is things are what they are and could have been so much worse. Many people would be grateful to have my problems instead of the ones they have. I'm upright (way upright) every day, fully functional, and for that I cannot express my gratitude to whatever has brought me this far.

So now, after lots of mindfulness training, I try to see pain as a gift. It reminds me of what I can handle, that I can get through anything if I have to. Without all this mess how would I have known what I was made of? That being said, if they invented a way to fix this tomorrow and the side effect was growing a tail, I'd be the first in line. But there's always an upside to everything. I am now exempt from vacuuming and heavy lifting. Neil was with me for the last surgery and over the past five years he's shown me what he is made of and the value of that gift has no measure. Now there will be new challenges with foreign doctors, different treatments and, of course, new ways of coping with pain (wine, pastries, French countryside). I try to take each day as it comes and stay hopeful that something new and helpful is on the horizon. While I'm waiting maybe a new life in France is just what the doctor ordered.

THE DEVIL IS IN
THE DETAILS

Living the dream. Now there's a phrase I've been hearing a lot these days. At this point it still feels like a dream, some surreal concept that doesn't quite belong to me. Even with the house deal signed and half our furniture gone, it hasn't quite sunk in yet. The super shopper lady returned today with her movers and as the treadmill was rolled down the driveway, I had no sense of this actually coming to pass. I think I'm still in the infatuation phase with this dream life.

This is the part where everything is romantic. All that's needed is an Edith Piaf CD to cue the movie in my head: me cycling up the hill in Semur to visit the little *épicerie* for fresh strawberries and thick white asparagus which I place in the basket of my vintage bicycle along with a bouquet of sunflowers. I'm wearing my jaunty French beret and a Givenchy Audrey Hepburn dress as I ride past an accordion player on the corner who serenades me with a perfect version of *La Vie En Rose*. I wave to him and, in perfect French, call over my shoulder, "Ah, Jacques, what a glorious day! Your music is like wine to the thirsty soul." Then Neil comes rushing in the room frantic about his travel visa. Fade to black.

There's fantasy and then there's reality. We both have to-do lists as long as one of my bandy legs. Everything from passports to Pap smears has to be dealt with before we leave. The visa drama has revealed that in order for Neil to stay in France for more than three months he actually has to fly to Montreal for a 15-minute meeting where he'll need to produce everything from our marriage certificate to fingerprints. Daily calls to Air Canada have become routine as we are still trying to get on the same flight. We still have to finish renovating and deal with the sale of the house, arrange for transatlantic shipping of the few things we are taking, stock up on things we can't get once we're there and try to see all of our friends before we go. Immigration policy must be studied, on and on. Of course this is all fine for me but Neil is still working full time between World Cup matches and golf opens.

I know how this sounds. Oh how she suffers, the toil and trouble just to get a new life in France. True, if this is my only problem in life things are pretty good. But to be honest it's the details that scare me. They remind me of how many challenges we will face in a new land. Every now and then I worry that such big changes will affect the marriage I hold so dear. Everyone keeps telling me how brave this is, but late at night, when sleep eludes me because I'm reviewing my list for the next day, I feel the anxiety creeping in and courage seems a long way off. I tell myself that somehow everything on the list will get crossed off and that we'll go whether we're ready or not. I have to. Jacques is waiting for me.

JESUS MISSUS, YOU'RE AN AWFUL HEIGHT

This is what a man in a bar in Newfoundland said to me one night. He left the bar alone. Some years later my cousin introduced me to a man at the Ottawa Jazz Festival. He turned out to be a fellow Newfoundlander and stood about five foot six. His eyes followed me slowly from head to toe, and without so much as hello he said, "Jesus, look at the height of ya. My tongue would be dry halfway up your leg."

I've alluded to my excessive height a few times so here's the lowdown on the up high, a constant theme in my life. I've been an Amazon for as long as I can remember. I was born tall. I reached my final adult height of six feet at age 12. Not a day goes by without someone commenting on my size and every time I meet someone their first comment is usually about my body. Whenever someone describes me, it's the first thing they say: "You know her, tall, skinny, big mouth." I've learned to accept it, as any significant shrinkage is unlikely.

It seems most people would like to be taller than they are. They always say, "Oh you're so lucky, I wish I was as tall as you." No, they don't. Sure, in my view everyone could use a couple of extra inches, but this life as a giraffe has some clear drawbacks. I was always taller than everyone else at school, allowing me to secure plum school play roles like King Herod and Bully Number Two. I was clumsy and awkward and fell down a lot, once while roller-skating in my mother's ceramic tile foyer, but I had that one coming. I still hit my head frequently, with my most recent moment of elegance seeing me smack headfirst into a stone doorframe, knocking me and everything I was carrying to the ground so far below.

Clothing has always been a special challenge. There's a petite store on every corner but usually only one tall store that sells giant polyester pants with waistbands that extend to my armpits. When I was young I had to be crafty. I collected boots of every style and color to cover my flood pants. Even now I have to be content with a wardrobe that fits me rather than one I like.

I occasionally wish to be a small woman. I'm always fascinated by the way men deftly carry women about in the movies. I picture Neil trying to romantically sweep me off my feet, him sweating and panting, his back breaking, my hands and feet dragging across the ground. What a mess. I would love to have small, feminine feet. Mine are like pontoons, which I suppose is necessary to prevent me from falling face-first on a regular basis. I longingly gaze at women with those beautiful pixie haircuts but I know I would end up looking like a giant Q-Tip. But there are some advantages. I can reach every shelf at the grocery store, handy for me and for the five foot nothing person who is somehow always shopping alongside me. I can see at concerts and I rarely get lost in a crowd. I can gain 20 pounds before anybody notices, which will likely come in handy in the land of *croissants*.

I am a bit worried about fitting in, no pun intended, in my little French town. Here in Canada I have many lovely Amazon friends but in Semur the ladies are regular size. If anything, they are quite petite. I don't want some Frenchman at my door expecting me to help him chop firewood because he heard a Canadian lumberjack had arrived. Maybe they'll see it as exotically attractive and intriguing. Or at least something not worth selling tickets to see.

I SURRENDER

I've been at war with my hair since about 1990. It's Texas hair, thick as rope and grows at an alarming rate. It's unruly and expands in all directions like a big ball of cotton candy as soon as the humidity goes above 50 percent. I coasted through the '80s like someone straight out of an episode of *Dallas*, spiral perm and all. It was big and swallowed my face whole, but it was stylin' at the time so I was golden. Then two disasters struck. The world decided that thin, silky hair was all the rage and the genetic blessings of my parents revealed themselves. Enter the premature grey.

And so began two decades of attacking roots with every chemical in the beautician's arsenal. I once had to have all the color stripped from my hair after a stylist, high at the time, accidentally dyed it Superman blue-black. My scalp was covered in scabs and it was a year before my hair colour resembled something from nature. Sadly, that wasn't the most painful aspect of this nonsense. I figure that over the last 20 years I've spent about $45,000 on my head. I'm absolutely serious. Good to know but I wish I'd made a large cocktail before taking out the calculator. And yet I was completely panic-stricken to hear that while the French do bread better than anyone in the world, hair colour is apparently not their forte. I emailed some ladies I know in France only to discover the horrible truth. Apparently, I'd have to drive 45 minutes to and from Dijon and pay a small fortune for color that might be something like what I'm used to. I've mentioned that I quit my job. I'll be trying to learn French and starting a new career as well as adjusting to a new culture and maybe trying to make a friend or two. How the hell does this hair business fit in?

But it seems I'm becoming practical in my middle age, a nice balance to the uncontrollable sagging and wrinkling. I decided enough was enough. The minute I handed in my letter of resignation I laid down my weapons of grey destruction and let nature take its course. Honest to god, I would have created less of a stir if I'd told people I was joining a cult. I was stunned by the strong reactions to this seemingly trivial decision. So I did some research and apparently this is actually a strange thing to do. There's even a whole website devoted to supporting women in their decision to abandon hair dye and entire debates about this as a feminist issue. Is this not the Oprah generation run amok? "You'll look old," they say. "You'll look tired," they say. Well, I'm sort of old and I'm definitely tired, so this will work out just fine.

And it was fine, until I went for one last haircut. Within two minutes of entering the salon, I was surrounded, lost in a sea of perfectly highlighted heads. I heard a faint battle cry in the distance and I began to waver. I sat in the waiting area with the colour conflict raging in my head while across from me sat a startlingly beautiful woman, one of those women who mystify me with their seemingly effortless style. Her hair? A perfect shade of pewter with chrome highlights. I showed her my skunk stripe and she assured me that this two-tone, bingo-babe madness would pass soon enough. She told me going grey would be one of the best decisions of my life and she predicted I'd be as fabulous as she was. I won't, but sweet of her all the same. And then she said, "I'm your sign to do it."

And "do it" I did. Armed with a steely resolve I sat for the last time with my revered hairstylist, Claude. I glanced back at the Silver Fox and I thought who has time to wait for things to pass? This was no time for cowardly retreat. I took a long look at my shoulder length mass of processed hair and said, "Cut it off." Claude, who lives for the dramatic makeover, practically levitated with joy. He snapped a shiny new blade in his long-handled razor and, quite wisely, spun me away from the mirror. Fifteen minutes later he turned me around to face my spiky silver hair.

They say a woman who cuts off her hair is about to change her life. This scarecut says I am too busy changing my life to give a rat's ass about peroxide and flat irons. I have been liberated from my hair and there is peace in the valley. It seems small, but maybe a global cease-fire isn't far off.

Love it and Leave It

I've never been very patriotic. I marvel at the flag-waving Americans pledging allegiance to the republic left, right and centre. They always say that the USA is the best country in the world, and maybe it is. Certainly the Big Gulp at 7-Eleven and next-day delivery from Zappos shoes puts them high on any list. But as I prepare to leave Canada and live in France under my British passport, I've been considering this country of mine.

I've been trying to think about the things that make up Canada besides hockey and Molson products. Tim Hortons (like Starbucks, only with higher levels of devotion), maple syrup, Great Big Sea, loonies and toonies,

David Suzuki, the Trans-Canada Highway, Anne Murray, the CBC, the RCMP, the Gordons (Pinsent and Lightfoot), k.d. lang and my personal favourite, Shoppers Drug Mart (like Walgreens or Boots on speed). I always think of Canada as a very civilized nation, a country that is humble and intelligent; fresh, clean and full of people who love canoeing and say they're sorry when someone else bumps into them. We have no history as fascists or dictators and no matter what evil plans Prime Minister Stephen Harper may enforce, I think we can all agree he's no Mussolini. We are relatively peaceful in the world and we don't kill criminals for killing other people. Plus, we made that space shuttle arm thingy. But when *The National* proudly presents Peter Mansbridge trying to look hot while stirring the nation into panic and the CBC is no longer distinguishable from CNN, it's time to go.

Maybe I'll miss Canada more than I anticipate. I'll be sitting in a café in France, a *pain au chocolat* in one hand, a fine Chablis in the other, turn to Neil and say "Aww, remember when the Conservatives raised the Goods and Services Tax, slashed Planned Parenthood funding and cut health care to the bone? Good times man, good times."

SOUR CREAM? REALLY?

I am in love with lists. I could not survive without the endless array of Post-it notes that are the only connection between everything in my head and the outside world. Luckily, I married someone who likes to talk in lists. Really, I'll say, "Neil, I can't help but notice that the garbage is still inside the house, why is that?" The reply will go something like this: "One, as you can see I'm very busy here on the couch watching *Gladiator*. B, I was waiting for the last piece of trash to be produced to maximize debris removal efficiency, and three, okay, I forgot." He counts it out on his fingers and it's hilarious. It's the mixing of the numbers and letters that I find especially amusing. We've been together long enough now to impose our habits on one another. He speaks perfect Newfanese and I speak perfect list. So when a friend asked me what I was going to miss the most, after family and friends, here's how it came out, in no particular order:

1)   English: The art of effortless communication. I can ask where the toilet is but I'm a long way from witty banter.

2)   My big shower: Europe is famous for shower stalls so small that no six-foot woman can shave her legs without crashing through the door, sustaining minor physical injury but major humiliation, and yes, I know this for a fact.

3)   Chinese and Mexican food: Not a Great Wall or Zapata's to be found in all of Burgundy. I'll have to suffer it out with French food.

4)   My own car: I have to share with Neil, never before attempted, and our French car is a standard, which I'm not sure I'll be able to drive. How can anyone drive a stick while eating and touching up mascara?

5)   Claude, my hairstylist: While he is responsible for my current state of near baldness, I'll still miss him.

6)   My super capacity washer and dryer: Three hours to wash four socks and two T-shirts in a tiny French washer.

7)   Convenience stores: Convenience in general. French stores close from noon to two-ish and have erratic hours in the evening and there's no such thing as one-stop shopping.

8)   My lovely doctor: I have no idea how to say, "Does this smell normal to you?" in French.

9)   Shoppers Drug Mart: Farewell, dear friend, with your aisles and aisles of happiness.

10) Sour cream: I will put it on anything and eat it from the tub with a spoon. To date, in a country that likely puts butter in the pavement, I have not been able to find it.

I'm sure once we get there we'll long for many things. But then I'm sure we'll find new French things that we can't seem to live without. I can only hope that the richness of the experience eclipses minor things. Living in a new culture surely outweighs big appliances, but if I can't find the sour cream I'm coming home.

THE ECONOMICS
OF HAPPINESS

Right off the bat I need to say that I stole that phrase from a book I just finished called *The New Good Life* by John Robbins. Robbins as in the Baskin-Robbins ice cream heir who read Walden, walked out on his family fortune and lived on essentially nothing. Then he made his own fortune only to lose it all at the hands of a fraudulent investment adviser. It's an interesting read about how we're attached to money and things and offers advice on how to simplify life and achieve richness of spirit. It fits very well with where my head is just now.

I often chronicle my time with Neil, almost 10 years now, in terms of decades. When we first met we were the '70s, free love, absolute abandon, nothing but groovy love morning, noon and night. Then came the '80s, acquisition all around: houses, cars, more houses, lots of cash and energy put into having shiny things. To quote Robbins, we were suffering from "affluenza." Then we were the '90s: debt, buyer's remorse and working like maniacs just trying to keep it all going. Ring in the '00s with reflection and questioning how we live and trying to figure out how to be fitter financially. Now in the '10s I am finally, finally debt-free and I feel the need to evolve, to try to live better with less and to measure happiness and success in a different way.

A very large part of running toward France is the quest for a completely different way of life. We will have far less income, actually about 70 per cent less. Over the next year my little adventure will require that I buy only the things I need instead of all the things I want. We will be renting so we will not pay a single dime of interest over the next year, for me, the first time since 1993. We are hoping to change the way we eat, more local and organic produce, maybe even try someday to grow some of our own food. Don't get me wrong, I'm not planning to change my name to Soleil and live on a farming commune disavowing all material goods. I just want to try living a simpler life.

While most of this is practical it also represents a philosophical shift for me. I grew up with the notion that money is safety, that success is defined by university degrees and a prestigious career. This no longer makes sense to me. Of course, it's certainly challenging to think about being dependent on my husband for money and I'm concerned about making it financially. But we've talked about this a great deal and we're a team, there's no his and mine. Well, except for the bathroom: mine. What makes sense to me now is really considering how I define happiness. Quality, not quantity. Experiences instead of things. Consume less and produce more. I wonder how many more books I'll have to buy to convince myself?

THE ECONOMICS OF REALITY

Well, so much for being philosophical, rambling on about living more with less, detaching from worldly goods and living the simple life. Ah, how Mother Earth of me, what a lovely little hippie I am. What a friggin' crock. Today all I can think is that I've actually lost it with this whole opposite life business.

Up to now I've been fine with it all. There really hasn't been much time to reflect on it. I've been in action mode, romanticizing the journey so much that I failed to notice that financing my way to France has left my bank account resembling that of a struggling student. To make matters worse, we finally received the shipping quote for the few things we are taking and I almost fell over from the shock of it. At first we assumed it was a mistake but no such luck. Apparently that is what it costs to ship a mattress, clothes, some artwork, a few odds and ends and a dozen or so French language books across an ocean. More motivation to separate the needs from the wants and the Great Canadian Purge continues.

Honestly, it's the world's slowest Band-Aid pull. It's like my life is being stripped away one little piece at a time. I actually gave away a pair of pants today, almost unheard of in the Amazon world. I confess, it's harder than I thought it would be. I suppose Neil is right, we don't really need the most beautiful toilet paper holder ever made, no matter how hard I fought that old lady at HomeSense for it. But every golf ball in the house is coming (I'm told they get lost a lot). By the time I'm done I'll be down to two pairs of underwear, any pants that are below my ankles and my computer. I know I need to stop this "poor me, off to France without all my knick-nacks" nonsense. Compared to Neil flying all the way to Montreal to get his visa only to find out that he didn't even need one, it's all pretty minor. Except for one thing.

Today I said goodbye to my longtime companion, my winter warrior, my ambassador of freedom. Today I handed my car keys to their new owner. Now he will enjoy the miracle of Bluetooth and XM radio and all wheel drive. He can go anywhere he wants whenever he wants while I have to politely ask Neil if I can use his car. How much oppression can one woman endure? I've been so spoiled in terms of transportation. Even before I had a licence I had a car waiting for me, so this is a very large shift. I really hope the marriage survives as we've already had a lively chat about who gets the car next Wednesday.

I know these things are quite trivial but today I'm consumed by doubts about this whole "simple life" business. I had to ask myself, do you really expect to pull this off? Don't you have any idea what a high-maintenance, complicated, neurotic person you are? You're a trained professional, for god's sake; can you not see that you are headed for absolute disaster here? Do something, anything to stop this foolishness. You can get a job at the Orange Julius up at the mall and be joyful right here in Canada. Richness of spirit, my arse. I want my car back.

SURREALITY

How bizarre my little life has become. Two months ago I was mired in the gritty business of running a locked psychiatric unit, but now it's just plain weird. I have no set schedule and no real structure to my day. It feels like it takes me hours to get around to actually doing anything halfway productive. The French study is down to learning one new word a day, incredibly useful words like *otage* (hostage) and *helice* (propeller). That's not to say that nothing is getting accomplished, Neil looks quite busy. I'm too preoccupied contemplating the surreal quality of my state of being to be of any use. Someone asked me the other day if I was excited about the big journey and I wasn't sure what to say. I don't feel excited. In fact, I don't feel much of anything at all. It could be that I have achieved some sort of state of enlightenment, a total detachment from all these changes. Or perhaps I'm so stressed that I have no insight into my own frozen state of terror. That's the trouble with being a psychiatrist; everything is always some sort of psychodrama that evolves out of endless analysis and interpretation.

I am well aware that I'm going somewhere. There's luggage everywhere I look. After the Purge the thing we own the most of now is luggage. There are strange men in my house putting things in a big wooden crate and Saran Wrapping my beloved mattress. I know that tomorrow I will leave this house forever but I have no real sense of this happening. It's one of the oddest experiences of my life.

I figure that I must be subconsciously casting it aside. Maybe it's just all too much for one little brain to take in, so it chooses to focus on frivolous matters like the minutiae of moving. Instead of succumbing to the anxiety of uprooting my entire life, I'm focused on coping with the disruption to my routine of daily living. The actual act of moving takes very little mental effort. We've done it so often now that we can actually pack, move, unpack and be set up with art hanging on the walls in 24 hours. For me the difficulty is the lack of a permanent and organized setup. I like having a place for everything in my life—towels here, husband there. And today that seems to be my only concern.

I'm not complaining about feeling so unaffected. I think it's far superior to running through the streets screaming, "ISN'T THIS EXCITING?!" I just find it curious. All I need to do now is figure out how to stop saying, "Hmm, how interesting, tell me more about that," to myself every time I have a thought about leaving. I'll have to learn to just let my thoughts come and go and do my best to keep moving forward. It'll hit me at some point. I just hope that I can get an appointment with myself when the denial dissolves.

Let the Games Begin

This is it, the first day of the rest of my life. Apparently, mid-life upheaval causes the use of tired clichés. The transatlantic launch is in about five hours. I'm here at an airport hotel, homeless and jobless but full of hope and determination. There's no turning back now, however, as everybody knows, an Air Canada delay would not be much of a surprise. So, passport? Check. Hockey bag jammed full of essentials from Rapid Release Tylenol to the riveting *501 French Verbs*? Check. Supportive husband? Check. Fear and dread? Check. In spite of all my squawking over the years about the importance of planning, I have no idea whatsoever how to do this. I have no clue what I'll be doing in this new property venture, what my days will look like, if I have the skills or aptitude for it or when I'm supposed to actually start working. I'm not even sure I want a job since unemployment seems to be going so well for me.

What kind of plan is this? Is there a manual of some sort and if so, will it be written in French? I function best with a well thought out strategy for most everything I do. I'm the person who actually reads the back of the shampoo bottle to see if two lathers are required. Today I feel lost without some sort of booklet outlining everything that happens immediately after I touch down in Paris. I know that my first three days in France will be spent at a bed and breakfast run by the people we plan to work with. What I really need is for them to greet me with a shiny brochure, one of those kit folders you get at open houses or conferences that has all the information you need neatly tucked inside; the steps to a successful new career and where to find a cheap bicycle made for a six-foot tall woman with limited neck mobility.

But as my mother always used to say, "What you wants and what you gets are two entirely different things." There's no step-by-step guide for this mid-life bedlam and I hope I don't fall apart because I don't have the manual for reassembly. Never mind, when we land there will be the fun of wading through the paperwork for Neil's residency permit, alerting the local authorities to our presence and then having the immigration medicals, which I hear are quite comprehensive. Maybe they give you wine and cheese before any orifice probing takes place, just to add a little class to the whole ordeal. At any rate, it's all part of the process and there's no getting around it.

And so ends our life as we know it. Who knows what's in store for us on the other side? Success or failure, laughter or tears, financial ruin or riches? As I step to the edge and leave one life for another I ask for nothing more than a little good fortune. Whether I'm walking away or walking toward, time will be the judge. For now, the only plan is one foot in front of the other.

~ And a New Life Begins ~

SEPTEMBER

Departures
and Arrivals

I'm great at coming and going; it's the in between that does me in. There are few things in life that displease me more than air travel. Of course Neil loves it. He thinks it's "fun" and he usually eats both our meals with gusto. There aren't enough drugs on the planet to put me to sleep on a plane but he's often out before we leave the tarmac. On this momentous flight he struck up a chat with a fellow who had been posted to Paris as an assistant to the Canadian ambassador. Next thing I knew, Neil and the diplomat were clinking wineglasses and ordering watches from the in-flight store like they were sorority sisters. At about the halfway point, the two of them were fed, watered and snoring peacefully, while I was on my third glass of wine trying to beat back the vision of plunging into the ocean. By the time we finally landed I was a wilted, dried-out pretzel of a woman, but my feet were on French soil. Where my luggage landed was anybody's guess.

Twenty-one hours to get from a hotel in Halifax to a bed and breakfast in Burgundy, so for me, bed was the operative word. For the next few days we were treated like the royalty we are with exquisite meals, cold *Crémant* in the cave by candlelight, the works. I spent my last morning there strolling around the gravel courtyard, the morning sun on my face and the family dogs at my heels. I thought this could be my new job, Lady of the Manor with the Labradors. I could just eat, drink, feed the dogs and occasionally hunt for pheasant wearing some kind of tweed ensemble, then later pull on a little Dior number for the bubbly in the cave. I'm nothing if not practical.

Our next stop was the tiny hamlet of Etrochey, home sweet temporary home, an old mill house restored by a local farmer and his wife. When we pulled up, I couldn't believe my eyes. We'd gotten an incredible deal on this place and I had to laugh at the irony of beginning a life as an unemployed layabout in a place such as this. The good news is that it's long paid for and all I have to do is avoid becoming attached to a spread that could only be mine if I were holding a winning lottery ticket. If this is the simple life, count me in.

Lowering
My Standard

I'm more the bookwormy, nerdy type, prone to excitement about themes in literature and whatnot. Math, I can't even talk about it intelligently. The good thing is I don't give a damn. I have Neil who can calculate the square root of 22,456 in his head, so why bother? There are competent engineers the world over who drool over principles of velocity and distance and whatever else goes on in physics books, so again, I leave those things to the experts. As for hand-eye co-ordination, I'm a disaster. I couldn't play a video game if my life depended on it.

But during the very first week of my new life in France my devil may care attitude has caught up with me. For a while now I've been avoiding driving the car we've rented on account of the three pedals and the funny stick between the seats. So I asked Neil if he'd be so kind as to offer me a little instruction, figuring after an hour or so I'd be zipping along the highway, passing every Peugeot and Citroën in sight.

Mon dieu there was less bucking and grinding in *Urban Cowboy*. And speaking of mechanical bulls, I've never seen poor Neil quite so pale. Ever since a couple of surgeons pieced my neck back together with plates and screws, one of my biggest fears in my life is a car accident and this stick-shift business isn't helping. All I can imagine now is desperately trying to remember what that third pedal is for as I am careening towards death on an icy curve. I know that many people love driving stick-shift cars and yes, I know it takes time to get it down, but I must say that I feel like a gangly puppet, hands and feet in perpetual motion with no hope of control. The secret is they make automatic cars that do all this for you. I know the stick devotees say that the joy of driving lies in the shifting but for me it lies in knowing that I, a highly distracted individual at the best of times, will not need to be doing four things at once on a steep hill in a foreign country. The remarkable thing is that I'm actually getting worse every time I drive. It's a wonder Neil hasn't had a heart attack or thrown up all over me from these rodeo rides. This can't go on for much longer in somebody else's vehicle as I'm not keen to call a Frenchman to inform him that I ripped out the transmission before leaving the driveway. I'll give it a few more tries but I might have to admit defeat. I guess it's not the end of the world, but how sad to be the lone loser in France who can't drive a stick. Maybe I was expecting too much from myself and I need to shift gears philosophically. Rome wasn't built in a day and building French Bobbi may take years.

THE FARMER
BRINGS A WIFE

Well, just as I had hoped, France has opened its arms and taken us in. Don't listen to those who tell you the French are cold and crusty, wary of the ugly North American. In less than two weeks we've met the warmest and kindest people imaginable. Maybe we've just been lucky and, to be fair, these are early days.

Enter The Farmer, Michel (think tall, dark Depardieu) and The Wife, Patricia, a tiny woman with a constant smile. They own the house we are staying in and have lovingly restored it from a ruin into something magnificent. They've thought of everything here, electronic shutters, lights above the river that cast a soft glow at night, comfy beds, a kitchen equipped with everything you could imagine, fresh flowers everywhere and plenty of wood for the fireplace. Beyond that they are incredible hosts. They welcomed us with a basket of farm fresh vegetables and eggs laid that morning. A few days later they came again to see how we were getting on and to invite us for dinner. Ooh dinner on a French farm, now this was something to be excited about. But then I saw myself sitting at the table, mute and feckless, nodding at anything that sounds familiar.

The perils of living in a new culture suddenly started smacking me in the face. What do people bring to a dinner here? What's impolite to talk about? Will I have to eat snails? And the big one, what to wear? I mean it's really hard to know. Last night the weather girl on TV was wearing skintight jeans and a tank top that failed to fully conceal a tatty black bra. Clearly her hair hadn't seen a brush in some time. If this is how she presents herself for all of France to see, what the hell does one wear for a farm dinner, burlap? Well, caution to the wind because this was it, my first invitation to a French house. I resolved to do the best I could and hoped the night wouldn't end in violence as a result of my inadvertently saying something ridiculously rude.

As is so often the case, my worry was pointless. The food was incredible with champagne and traditional *gougères* (cheese puffs to die for), red and white wine from the vineyards of Beaune to complement the simmered *lapin* (rabbit), zucchini and bacon casserole, local cheeses, then a pear tarte handmade by the Farmer himself. They are incredibly generous people and seemed so pleased to have us. They even had a map of Canada placed it on the table so we could show them where we were from.

I mucked about with the French and made several apparently hilarious errors but we must have done something right as they invited us back to finish the leftovers at lunch and to join them at a restaurant next week. I was relieved beyond description. I feared it would be next to impossible to ever meet anyone here, that Neil and I would spend all our time on our own and, naturally, proceed to kill each other. The thing is I know there are nasty, rude people everywhere, even in Burgundy, but we haven't found one yet. Still, we have many more people to meet and many more difficult situations to face. For starters, there's no sign of our stuff from Canada so I can say this: if my mattress and clothes don't get here soon, there'll be at least one crotchety, snarly woman in France.

A Sunday in Burgundy

It's only been a few weeks and already it seems like a lifetime ago that I left my home for this strange place. Each day is an endless stream of the unfamiliar. While on the surface many things seem the same, in reality it's like living on another planet. This past Sunday was yet another day of discovery.

We started with Michel and Patricia for lunch, which in French translates to champagne followed by more food than I've ever eaten for lunch in my life. The table looked like a buffet for a wedding. Again, the wine flowed, and it now seems likely that I'll spend the rest of my time here half in the bag. We sampled the feast and talked, or in my case listened, and we met their younger son, 16 and madly in love with his girlfriend of a week as evidenced by the frantic rate of texting between PlayStation sessions. It's somehow reassuring to find that a teenager in rural France is not so different from any of the Canadian kids I've met.

I've learned that the French Sunday lunch goes on for hours and finishes just in time for dinner. After eating myself into a stupor I was ready for bed, but visits to a local autumn fair and a village antique shop were proposed and who'd say no to that? I'd never been to a country fair in my life and I assumed it would be a lot like any other in the world, but for me any outing in France is a marvel, especially when I'm slightly intoxicated. The locals were milling about, chatting and double kissing, admiring the regional fare, like honey from the flowers in the Alps and fragrant goat cheese while the kids rode ponies. But the real treat of the afternoon was a chainsaw sculpture competition. Even the woodsmen here appreciate art.

The country antique store was a place frozen in time packed with beautifully restored armoires and dressers, vintage French postcards, old records and cameras from the 1930s, marble topped bistro tables, anything needed for a French movie set. The owner himself was like someone sent straight from French central casting with his jaunty scarf and a lit *Gauloise* dangling precariously from the side of his mouth the entire time we were in the shop. He was delighted to explain the history of all the pieces and was as friendly as everyone else we've met. We finished the day with a drive through the countryside, visits to a small vineyard and a few pretty villages and then home again right at wine o'clock.

Now that's what I call a Sunday. I know they won't all be this wonderful but for now I'm happy to delude myself that this is my new weekend ritual. Of course, I'll be 320 pounds and in alcohol rehab, but hopefully speaking much better French.

THE VILLAGE IDIOT

Speaking of speaking, a language update is in order. If only I knew how to say "I suck" in French. With all the time it takes to enjoy France and to set up a life in a foreign country, my French study has dwindled significantly. I have a habit of this kind of thing, procrastinating whenever increased effort makes the most sense. One would think that now that I'm actually here, learning French should be the top priority, conjugation and *vocabulaire* day and night. But no and there's a price to be paid.

The other night at the dinner on the farm, I had several opportunities to display my ignorance. I was asked what my plans were for tomorrow, to which I replied, "Yes." Patricia laughed and again asked, "No, what are your plans for tomorrow?" patient and smiling as always. I answered, "Yes, thank you." Everyone laughed, including me. I mean really, what else can be expected? These things take time so I'm not too worried about such minor offences.

A little later I gathered my courage and jumped into the current topic of discussion, Sarkozy and his plans for France. I began carefully and was surprised by how well I was doing. Suddenly the words flowed out smoothly unhindered, remarkably unlike my usual halting, painfully slow speech. I gradually worked up to my typical motor mouth pace and thought, now I'm cooking. I'm a genius, immersion personified. It was at that exact moment I noticed the confused faces at the table and I felt Neil tapping me on the leg. Don't stop me now man, can't you see I'm on a roll? I carried on but again the leg tapping, and by then I couldn't help but notice that Neil was regarding me with that all too familiar simultaneous look of amusement and pity. "Bobbi, my love, you're speaking English." And I was, which accounts for how well I was doing. But I'm sure this happens to everyone.

As I'm quite famous for letting whatever comes into my head fall unfiltered out of my mouth, it's not such a bad thing for me to stop and reflect a little on what I am about to unleash into the world. While I managed to laugh the whole thing off, I must admit that I did feel entirely dimwitted. I really hope I don't become the goofy Canadian providing amusement for the French folks as I travel from town to town. Although, if it pays well enough …

HIDDEN PLACES

Exploration is a funny thing. The thrill of discovering a new place, a new culture, a new way of living is part of the collective experience that makes us truly feel alive. In my days as a psychiatrist, I was a master of the internal expedition. Of course one occupational hazard, and there are many, is endless self-analysis that apparently doesn't stop the minute you sell off the couch and set up abroad. The explored life offers much about the world but perhaps even more about us. I've learned that I can walk away from everything I know and be okay (so far); that I can adapt. In fact, if we take speaking French out of the equation, I'm often quite pleased with how I'm doing here. But I'm also discovering dark caves within myself that I never knew existed. And there are times when wandering around in your own head can be a dangerous endeavour.

The other day, Neil and I went to the French immigration office in Dijon so he could begin the application for residency. We walked into a bland office filled to the rafters with people from all over the globe. It was dank and depressing and smelled like a mix between a well-used toilet and a greasy restaurant. Everyone looked so weary, so beaten down by life and death and poverty and who knows what else. I felt every pair of eyes on me, the obviously advantaged, "never seen a day of war in her life" woman. What I also couldn't help but notice was that besides my redheaded husband, I was the only white person in the place. I don't often think about the colour of my skin but on this day I thought about white a lot.

I've spent my entire career working with the poor and neglected people of our world. I consider myself to be a person well-versed in the ills of social injustice and a dedicated soldier in the war against oppression and inequality. I support Amnesty International and V-Day. Neil and I both sponsor women in the Congo and Rwanda. Yet my first thought was that I didn't belong here with the asylum seekers; that there must be another office for healthy, educated, people who have registered retirement savings plans. It was my first glimpse of my own unexamined sense of middle class Canadian entitlement. I was thoroughly shocked, swiftly ashamed and felt like a complete fraud. For all my donations and advocacy and all the other bullshit I get on with, I have no idea what it means not to be geopolitically privileged, nor do I have any notion of real suffering.

What I learned from this is that true exploration requires a map to all the lovely parks and monuments but also one for the ugly backstreets and slums. This shame opened my eyes and my heart. I need to learn to be prepared for the good and the bad on this journey. So bring it on I say. I'm ready for the next slam to the system, the next discovery, no matter how hard it is to look at. It can't be all about wine and charming villagers now can it?

OCTOBER

TOUR DE FRANCE

Meanwhile I am moving forward in my quest for this much talked about simpler life. I've dropped out of the rat race, as they say, and one thing I've noticed so far is how much I enjoy the freedom from traffic. These days getting stuck behind a slow moving tractor is as bad as it gets. I still miss my car but I am exploring alternative modes of transportation. As I said, I've had some pretty wild fantasies about life in France including zipping around town on a *bicyclette*. Well, fantasy and reality are closing in on each other, as I am now the proud owner of the best French bicycle ever made. Initially, I was insistent on a vintage bicycle complete with a wicker basket and a shiny bell, but in a rare fit of rational thought and consideration of practicalities I went for the Gitane E-bike.

Now this beauty does have the required basket for pretending that I'm Audrey (Hepburn, Tautou, either one will do) but instead of romantic wicker it's black metal, which I have to say is a far better choice for wet weather (because I so love to ride a bike in the rain) and for holding several heavy bottles of wine, so clever me. But the genius of this bicycle is the switch on the left handle. One press of a button and, like magic, a battery charged motor kicks in to assist the pedals. It's like having Lance Armstrong hidden in your backpack ready to spring out when you hit a steep hill. Semur has many daunting inclines and I was more than a little curious as to how my 42-year-old pins would carry my equally old arse to the bakery. With this machine, I'll be unstoppable.

So today I took it out for a test spin, inspired by visions of the wind blowing through my hair as I effortlessly travelled mile after country mile, movie star meets Olympic cyclist. Of course I'd forgotten that I had scrapped my long blonde hair for the spiky scarecut, so by the time I got home I looked less like Catherine Deneuve and more like Billy Idol. I also forgot that I haven't been on a bike since I was 15 so I mostly weaved about like a toddler in need of training wheels. And speaking of old arses, mine is so sore from the ride that I can hardly sit down. So much for my hopes for the yellow jersey this year.

What is quite intriguing here is that when people (mostly the men) ride bikes, they gear up with as many complicated cycling *accoutrements* as possible. They wear aerodynamic racing helmets, special cycling shoes and wildly patterned lycra shorts and shirts, I mean it's serious business. I must have been quite the sight in my sweats and clogs. Never mind, the next time I hit the road I plan to sidle up to these cycling snobs, kick into electric mode and yell, "Eat my dust, fellas!" as I rocket into the ditch.

LOST AND FOUND

Finally, yesterday morning came the call that a truck would be arriving to Etrochey in fifteen minutes. Not just any truck but one with clothing, Neil's Big Mac work computer and of course, our beloved mattress. Needless to say, this was exceedingly welcome news 13 days beyond the expected date. Neil had been wearing the same three T-shirts and two pairs of pants for weeks and had one lightweight jacket, not at all suitable for the now chilly autumn nights. But who cares about him? He's irrelevant and inconsequential. It's all about me, and I want my mattress.

Neil went out to meet the truck, which could not (later revealed would not) come all the way to the front door. Of course it was pouring rain. Now, let me just say that we paid extra for air shipping so that there would be no delay, and as well for the distinct pleasure of having someone gently place our items inside the house. I know this because it's printed quite clearly in a contract I signed.

I was preparing to make coffee for the hefty French *hommes* who would soon be tracking mud all over the house, but after about half an hour of nothing going on I decided to see what the hold-up was. I went out and was shocked to see my husband of few words fully engaged in a very animated conversation with one really skinny man. I use the word man loosely as he appeared to be about 16 years old. But imagine my relief when I saw that the *garçon* had brought his trusty helper, a young lass dressed to go out dancing, heels and all, his girlfriend, who had come along for the ride. *Mon Dieu.*

Apparently the *garçon* was not remotely prepared to unload the goods, had no way of cracking open our large wooden crate and was less than pleased that we kept waving a contract at him. I could actually see my beloved mattress in the back of the truck and it was all I could do to not push everyone aside so I could drag it out and flop down on it in the middle of the street. But I refrained, as suddenly the *garçon* became quite enraged and started violently jumping on the crate, which seemed to do the trick. I must remember that unbridled rage is the solution to every problem. Then he started tossing the boxes one by one into the street. *Merde.* Neil and I had to carry the now wet and mushy boxes all the way down to the house. For some reason the moving company had repacked everything so I had no idea of what was where. Customs had ripped open several boxes creating several deep slices through the contents, and we found Neil's level (apparently a crucial item for a life in France) sticking out the back of a valuable painting. I assume it was these little extras that cost so much.

As I waded through the carnage, I noticed the two wardrobe boxes with my clothes were missing. We looked and looked but they were nowhere to be found. Of course the golf clubs and all of Neil's clothes so easily found at the Gap made it. My years of trolling the world for pants flashed before my eyes and immediately grief began to set in. Insurance was little consolation in this case. Never mind the time, where the hell would I find the strength for clothes shopping that for a giraffe like me in a foreign country would border on lunacy? I kept saying over and over in my head, things don't matter. Then I would remember my Max Mara cuffed black dress pants found years ago in Rome or my grey linen ones not even worn yet and I had to fight back the tears.

Several hours later, after everything was accounted for, I found two flat misshapen boxes tucked in a corner. Like a savage I ripped them open and sweet salvation lay within. I swear I heard choirs singing. So much for detachment from possessions. Having experienced the loss for even a short time has confirmed that the simple life is one where I wear the pants in the family.

FALLING IN LOVE AT LE CHEVAL ROUGE

Already we've had the definitive French experience and no words can truly capture it. Like the time I stood before Botticelli's *Birth of Venus* in Florence or after reading *The Stone Diaries* for the first time, I have stored it in my memory museum so that I can revisit it again and again. It was the absolute embodiment of why I wanted to come to France and everything I love about this amazing culture.

Michel and Patricia graciously invited us to dine with them and a few friends at a local restaurant. Again, ecstasy then agony. What to wear? How not to speak rapid English while believing that perfect French is flowing out of my mouth? How to make sure I order something that doesn't have brains in it? How to try all the wines and not be totally hammered before the first course? All this was swirling around my already busy melon for a couple of days. Of course the dinner was scheduled to begin at eight o'clock on the evening of the day of our moving debacle. I was exhausted and still recovering from the I-almost-lost-all-my-pants trauma.

The lovely farmer collected us before we met up with the others. He said, "We are nine tonight," and I started sweating. How the hell will I understand a word once they all get yakking top speed? I'll be a completely drunk doofus, smiling, nodding and eating rare brains. We met everyone outside, Patricia and her three longtime girlfriends, a husband and son as well as the other son of Michel and Patricia, Gaëtan, a chic young man who greeted us in English, allowing me to exhale a little. A quick scan of the crowd revealed that I was dressed appropriately, thank you again gods of French etiquette.

Le Cheval Rouge is a lovely little place attached to a large patio and bar owned by a woman about fifty, funky and French to the core, who knew this crowd well. Gesturing and talking at a wild pace, she handed out the extensive menus and I saw all the gastronomic treasures of Burgundy before me. While the food and wine were spectacular, the big love was to be found in the company.

First the ladies. Patricia brought along her English dictionary and explained to her friends that they would need to talk slowly and they did, all night. They asked me questions about Canada and they complimented my hair. One of them thought the colour so lovely that she didn't believe it was natural. They helped me order and best of all said I had little accent and that my French was quite good, liars all but still. They talked about their friendship that spanned over 40 years and they were charming beyond description. Their warmth and kindness was something to behold.

Then the men. To my left, Philippe, identified to me as soon as I sat down as a *farceur*, and he was indeed hilarious in any language. He too talked very slowly to me all night and offered me tastes of his meal. Gaëtan spoke his newly learned English with Neil and was clearly taking an opportunity to make his father proud. Then there was Michel, seated at the head of the table, choosing and tasting the wine, suggesting what to order and taking the first bite of food: a sweet king holding court. He was beaming all night, so proud of his son speaking English with his foreign guests. He paid for the entire meal as a celebration of the end of the rental season of the house that we were so lucky to have found. He is a gentle giant and one of the loveliest men I have ever encountered.

The lady who owns the restaurant served us all night and she was nothing short of a one-woman comedy show. Neil asked for his meat medium rare and she guffawed loudly and barked, "NON! You are in France now, there is no in between!" When I asked about the debate raging in France over retirement age and pensions, things got really exciting. The volume rose, the pace picked up, everyone was talking at once and gesturing madly, the young guys were rolling their eyes, it was fantastic. Neil winked at me across the table as we sat back and took it all in. The evening was so congenial, so full of laughter and *bonhomie* that by the end it had become one of the best of my life.

At one point I had quietly asked Patricia if it was rude to taste food from one another or to use *tu* instead of *vous*. She gave me her huge smile and said that when with friends this is the thing to do. Then she said to me, "*Et Bobbi, tu es avec tes amis*"—you are with your friends. I don't care how long it takes to get a bank account or that automatic cars are as common as unicorns, I am falling in love with France and, for at least one night, France loves me too.

HELL HATH NO FURY
LIKE A WOMAN SILENCED

I might just have to slap my husband out of his shock because I, famous for non-stop blabbity-blah, have become practically mute. In the last four weeks, apart from the recent outings with our hosts, I've said almost nothing to anyone outside my house and it's making me slightly wiggy.

Just in case it seems like nothing but dewy delight and happy rays of sunshine over here, it is not. Sure, we have managed to start putting things together. We bought a cheap car that I can drive, the standard now abandoned at Neil's gentle suggestion. We opened a bank account, bought a house and we have French cellphones—so far, so good. About that house thing, yes, less than a month in and we made an offer on a house, well, a roof and four walls. How this one plays out remains to be seen. But the point is that all these important events have taken place without me saying much beyond *bonjour* and *au revoir*. And today I've had my fill of it. I'm frustrated with major things being arranged and then hearing the translation in the car 20 minutes later, a poor concubine being shuttled about.

I've been too busy getting settled to be able to co-ordinate with my French teacher who is currently a 45-minute drive away from me. Now one could surmise that if I spent more time practising French and less time writing about the mundane details of my life, I could *parlez-vous* the ding-dong in no time. The real issue is that I have no plan, no structured way to go about it. Teaching myself from books and CDs is a good start, but so far it's slow going to say the least. Also, I don't think watching French dubbed *Law & Order* every night is working out as well as I'd hoped. Apparently, there's not much call for perfectly enunciated, "In the criminal justice system, the people are represented by two separate yet equally important groups," out here in the country. Too bad, because it's the only thing I can say with a perfect French accent.

The user guide for my cellphone is bilingual but sadly the second language is German. I can't understand the manual for my new bicycle. Because I'm the one with official residency here, everything is in my name and, even though all correspondence is addressed to me, it goes straight to the man who can actually read it. Now he just opens all my mail for me. If anyone calls I have to hand the phone to him. Can cutting my meat for me be too far off?

It's downright vexing to be a full-grown person and suddenly realize that you have the independence of a five-year-old. I suppose it's not a bad deal having other people handle everything for you. Maybe this is what life is like for the diva *du jour* but without all the jet-setting and perfect thighs, it's all a bit defeating. I've decided the only cure for whining is wining, so I'm unpacking the big glasses tonight. But first I have to get through the grocery store. My plan is to saunter up to the meat counter and when the sweet gal asks me what I would like, I will confidently proclaim, in flawless French, "The police who investigate crime and the district attorneys who prosecute the offenders. These are their stories."

WRECK SWEET WRECK

I mentioned a house. It seems that old habits do indeed die hard. The upshot of doing something totally ridiculous is that it gives you a new standard by which all future stupidity can be measured. No matter what shenanigans go on in my life, I can always say, "Your Honour, I realize it was entirely naïve for me to think that I wouldn't get caught but compared to the time I bought that wreck in France, this is nothing." Now the wise thing to do would be to live a while in France, see how I like it, ease into the culture, blah, blah, le blah. Instead, why not buy a roof, four walls and some dirt floors from a Parisian *artiste* and then embark on a full-scale renovation without even knowing how to say the word hammer?

Those who know me will not be surprised. I can actually hear the rolling of eyes and the sighs of the wise, those who know full well that two months into this I'll be pulling out what's left of my hair. The only redeeming feature of this place at the moment is that the finished space would be about 800 square feet, so it fits with trying to live with less. But it will be quite a challenge, both in terms of design and a very tight budget. Anyway, the offer has been accepted but the papers are still not signed, so who knows? But paperwork and practicalities aside, I couldn't help but be absolutely amazed by how cozy yet luxurious this house is. Why, all I need to do is open the wine and relax. This may be the day that all the marbles have actually been lost.

A Life in 15
Items or Less

It seems that between grappling with *la grammaire* and buying houses I spend a lot of my time at the grocery store. Well, I like to eat and I'm in the country; it's either that or cow-tipping. It's also one of the few things I can do without an interpreter. I did try to mail a letter by myself the other day which didn't go well and is a story for another day.

So there I was, fashionable as ever, sweatpants, knobby pilled fleece and bedhead, more beast than beauty. I was trying to get in and out quickly as I suspected that I might have smelled worse than I looked. There was a woman ahead of me clearly in some sort of panic, whipping items along the belt with frenetic speed. She reminded me a lot of my former too busy self so I turned my attention to the couple behind me.

They were about 80, this husband and wife who stood somewhere between my waist and my shoulder, as many people in France do. While they were immaculately dressed and groomed, they didn't seem especially wealthy. As they slowly and carefully placed each item on the belt, I couldn't help noticing what they had. Huge figs, specialty cheeses, two bottles of Burgundy wine and a bottle of sherry, fresh *baguettes*, fine coffee, berries, *crème fraiche*, huge eggplants and tomatoes, fresh fish, veal chops, duck breast and dark chocolate. Their last item was my favourite, a huge gold can of aerosol hair spray, one that I recognized from my grandmother's time. It seemed to me that the history of their life was laid before me on this conveyor belt. A lifetime of fine food and wine. A wedding supper, lunches for children, holiday feasts, summer picnics, rationing during wartime, treats for grandchildren, funeral buffets, all served with perfectly styled hair. These two weren't buying much food but what they had was the very best. Each item was so lovingly taken from the cart that it was really one of the best things I've seen here so far.

It got me to thinking about how much we can tell about people from their items at the checkout. I often have a feeling of being quite exposed when all my sundries are out there for the world to see, but hopefully others don't read as much into a grocery cart as the average psychiatrist does. What

I saw here was that this couple's life could well have been the life I had dreamed of living for so many years. Did they feel blessed to be surrounded by some of the best food in the world enjoyed over five-hour lunches? Or is it simply all they've ever known and so not a matter for reflection or gratitude? Was this a life, like so many, simply taken for granted?

I had these same thoughts when I first saw Paris. I wondered how anybody ever gets through a workday there without being overwhelmed by the beauty of the city. In my head I know that the daily routine of life has a way of blocking out the spectacular and awe-inspiring sights around us. But my heart wants to believe that each day every Parisian stops to admire something and has their breath taken away.

I want to thank this couple for reminding me to appreciate everything around me while I'm here, to try and experience each moment in France as a gift. I also want to thank them for not judging me too harshly as my life was also laid out on the conveyer belt: four big bags of Lay's chips.

THE SWEET SMELL OF SUCCESS

With all that's been going on, I have badly neglected my skin care regime, which usually consists of nail clipping and the occasional smear of body lotion. All things considered, supple skin is hardly a priority right now. But once I became scaly enough to be officially classified as a reptile, it was time to get a move on. I couldn't find a loofah at the grocery store and the pharmacy was selling foot files for 16 euros (about $22 CDN), so I knew I could no longer avoid venturing into the world of French beauty boutiques. I'd been dreading it for a couple of reasons. I am desperately trying to steer clear of spending opportunities (and oh how I love these stores) and I have no idea how to ask for a foot file and loofah in French. Neil, always so helpful, said, "You know, if you'd looked these words up in the dictionary before you came, you'd know what to ask for." Oh, it must be so wonderful to be right all the time. Anyway, there's a chain store next to the supermarket called Beauty Success. I ventured in, and lo and behold, here in the middle of the country is a store that sells the complete line of Chanel, Dior and Lancôme make-up and every lotion and cream ever made. Bananas and state of the art skin care in the same place—what a country.

Too excited to be concerned about language, I walked straight up to the gorgeous 19-year-old salesgirl (made up within an inch of her life) and started the drama of telling her what I wanted. After ten minutes of my painful speech and violent gesturing, including a pantomime of a complete body exfoliation, she handed me a loofah mitt. And what is it called? A "loofah." I won't be telling my *Monsieur* that one. Again, like everyone we meet, the girl was incredibly polite and at the checkout she tossed a bunch of perfume samples in the bag, 12 to be exact.

Which brings me to my actual point. France is obsessed with fragrance. Everything here has some sort of scent. The men are drowning in it and the women are worse. Even the cars are made with different fragrances. It's impossible to find any kind of soap or laundry detergent without some assaultive smell. Even the ones with a fragrance called soap would melt the hair right out of your nostrils. For some reason, I don't want my underwear to smell like honey and apricots, but that's just me. Coming from years spent in a strict scent-free environment, it's complete olfactory overload. I initially thought that the girl might have gone overboard on the samples because she thought I smelled bad. What I'm hoping is that she gave them to me because I smelled like nothing and she felt it her duty to Frenchify me a bit.

Who am I to argue with an entire culture? It's all part of the adjustment to a new life. Today I'm going to try out the latest perfume from super designer Thierry Mugler. The package describes it as a radiant, vibrating (I'd like to know how), mysterious scent. The best part is that it's called Alien. Me, I'm just hoping to stink like a local.

French Kissing

I know the key to living in another culture is to rise to the occasion and embrace, adopt or at least respect the way things are done. For the most part, I'm going along with everything, like not batting an eye when the entire nation goes on strike and riots in the streets causing 4000 gas stations to go dry. The French are all about revolution and the closer *Monsieur* Sarkozy gets to his pension reform the more revolutionary things become. We're rationing gas as instructed and by the end of this week I fear Mad Max will rule the highways of France, but I digress.

What I'm on about right now is all this kissing I have to do every time I see someone. I love it and I don't. At first it's charming and you instantly take on the air of a chic European. It's romantic in a sense and good for the ego to think that everyone you see wants a kiss from you. After a while it becomes a bit of work because the art of *les bises* is not as easy as it looks. First of all, it varies from place to place. Some areas dictate a single kiss on each cheek, some an alternating cheek triple play and the other day, I noticed women in the town going in for the quadruple. Who has time for that? Imagine going out for a night with the girls. It would be time to go home as soon as you'd finished saying hello.

Second, it's easy to misjudge as you're bringing your face in, one false move and it's full on mouth kissing someone you don't know or head-butting yourself, the other person or both of you into unconsciousness. Or in my case, awkwardly kissing the air as the person walks away. Trust me, there's no successful recovery move for this faux pas. Plus, and this could be the MD in me, but how the hell do you avoid the flu with all this kissing going on? No wonder France has the highest rate of antibiotic use in the world. If you lick everyone you meet you're bound to be a bit more germ infested than the average person. Okay, you don't actually lick people, so travellers please take note, but there is an awful lot of virus sharing potential.

I'm thinking of making a list of people I'm willing to kiss in an effort to save time and decrease cold medication expenditures. But then I think of that episode of *Seinfeld* where Jerry refused to kiss his neighbours and became a social pariah, probably not a good move in terms of blending in with the locals. On second thought, I'll keep on with it. It is lovely to stop and press your cheek to the warm face of another human being as a way of saying hello. It reminds me all the time that I live here now and I have to do things differently, and there's no time to spare. Sarkozy is about to raise the retirement age to 62, and in the spirit of cultural adaptation I'm off to set some cars on fire.

A Method
to this Madness

Word of the Wreck has gotten around to my crowd back in Canada and I must say the feedback is just as I expected, everything from silence to laughter to warnings about every disaster that could come my way during this process. My wise friend Monique, who is very familiar with my house fetish, summed it up perfectly: "What took you so long?" But I assured her that this is not some impulsive folly. I admit that this statement may not be a stellar example of self-awareness, but at the very least the purchase was discussed at length with people who have been successful in the French property market for some time. Right. One conversation should be more than enough to proceed with confidence.

We've been here before, a grand total of eight houses now ripped apart and pieced together again. Usually when we go at it we're like a runaway train, working full time at our day jobs, renovating and designing into the wee hours. We exist for months on grilled cheese sandwiches and instant noodles (he hammers, I cook) and run ourselves to the point of collapse. Then as soon as the paint dries we sell the house and congratulate ourselves on breaking even. Oh, but this time it'll be different (I say this every single time) as the people we're planning to work with will manage the entire project from day one.

Now the good thing is that this will be the ultimate on-the-job training experience for a life in French property. The not so good thing is that it will also be the ultimate marriage test. By the end of it I hope we won't be communicating solely through our lawyers. Here's my master plan: design the *merde* out of the house, move in and if for some reason I have to resort to a life of crime to make ends meet (there has to be a brothel out here somewhere), we'll turn it into a vacation rental and find somewhere else to live. So it's a risk, but at least a calculated and briefly considered one. I'm sure someone will remind me in four months that I said this.

We've already scoped out a few other projects in the area and *vive la différence*. Trades people, or *artisans* as they are called here, are highly trained and assume full responsibility for their work for a period of ten years. Imagine. They take pride in their work, are very respectful and so far not a plumber's crack in sight. Surely this is the way to go. I once came home to find two workmen covered in dust and grime sitting on my off white dining chairs, eating my food and watching my television. Everyone who has ripped up a house has horror stories and mine would take a day to tell. I've also worked with some phenomenal people but they took years to find, so there's no way I'd go solo in a foreign country and I wouldn't recommend it to anyone else either.

It might be a challenge for us to let someone else control things but it comes with a promise to keep the project on budget, something I've yet to achieve on any renovation. Oh, who am I kidding? I've never been in the remote vicinity of a budget so I'm dying to discover this bit of sorcery. Now there's no choice but to be sensible and frugal because once the money from the sale of our Canadian house is gone there's no more tucked away in a bank in Switzerland (Revenue Canada, please be advised). Of course, what I've bitten off far exceeds my chewing ability, but what else is new? And, of course, I'm nervous about all this. It could be an absolute disaster. But it could also be a dream come true. Who knows? Either way I'll be all right. If we get really short on cash I can always head up to a strip club in Dijon to audition for Stretch Mark and Cellulite Night. I could be wrong, but I think it's the grey hair that'll get me the gig.

Escargot Mail

Despite persistent rumours to the contrary, paper mail does actually still exist. There may even be a few people left on the planet who can write full sentences like, "My, that story is so funny," known to anyone born after 1990 as LOL. While I appreciate technology as much as the next person, I do mourn the decline of letter writing. There's something romantic about a well crafted letter. I think of the famous correspondence between Elizabeth Barrett and Robert Browning all those years ago and somehow Skype sex doesn't quite have the same cachet.

Certainly I've been up to my eyes in letters since arriving in France, but there's not a shred of romance to be found in the lot. Letters to prove that

I have been driving since I was 17, letters to and from banks and insurance companies, and the latest, letters to Orange, the major cellphone provider here. In order to get my account activated I had to mail contracts, passport copies, a letter from the bank and a cancelled cheque, so off to the post office I went. It was jam-packed so clearly not everyone is texting, emailing and ordering online 24/7. After consulting my handy phrase book, I confidently approached the counter, asked for an envelope and from there it went quite awry. She started talking top tongue, rapidly offering me all kinds of mailing options. I had no idea what to choose and I could hear the long line of people behind me sighing simultaneously. How the French must adore the millions of foreigners who descend upon them each year. I had no idea what to do so out of desperation I asked the woman behind me if she could help me. Again, my new life as a five-year-old.

Now she was no dummy, this one. "*Bien sûr Madame*," she said with a charitable smile. She quickly took all my papers and my pen and simultaneously passed all her post to the woman behind the glass. She filled out my envelope while chatting away with the post woman, passed mine through, took hers back and *voilà*, multitasking at its finest. I realize that by helping me she was speeding up the whole process for herself and everyone else but still, *très gentille* of her I think and at least I was able to thank her properly. But really it seemed like a huge endeavour to have to gather papers, drive to the post office and do the verbal tango to get such a simple job done.

I now realize how my Canadian life has shaped a dependency on lightning fast transactions, everything from shopping to banking. Here, there's no such thing as a bank teller, instead there's a receptionist who arranges an appointment for you to meet with a banker for anything and everything. It sounds prolonged, and it is, and seems incredibly outdated to me. But maybe it's not such a bad thing to be forced to slow down and actually sit with people face to face to discuss things in a civilized manner. It will take some getting used to and I'm not widely known for my patience, so we'll see how it goes. I'm hoping I don't have some sort of public "I've been waiting forever" episode that requires alerting the French authorities to a Canadian giraffe rampage. The only up side is it that once the police got there, I know they'd decide I wasn't worth the four hours of paperwork.

WRECKING OVARIES

As for my own paperwork, the sale documents for the Wreck have been signed and the key has been handed over, which is quite amusing since the house has no back door. And so begins a seven-day cooling off period during which a mad scramble must ensue to determine if we can make it work within our modest budget. After the seven days are up there's no turning back.

Where shall I find the strength for this escapade? I'm still not recovered from my last renovation. I think my house in Canada was finished in the middle of July so that's about three months ago. For some reason it feels like a fair bit has gone on since then. Oh yes, all that relocating to a foreign country business. I knew there was a reason why I feel as decrepit as this house. When I left Canada I swore up and down, literally, that there was no way I was getting into another renovation for at least a year or two and—stamping of feet now—maybe never again. It turns out I'm a home-owner and a liar.

I'll need all the guts and grit my little gonads can produce because I'll admit that I'm more than a little anxious about this one. You'd think by now that I'd be able to do it in my sleep and intellectually, no problem. It's the emotional part that gets me every time. The stress of upheaval, the long hours, the never ending choices that have to be made, not that a full day of deciding where to put electrical outlets isn't a riveting and entertaining way to spend one's time. I'm not a fan of mess and disorder and yet it's the only consistent thing in my life. My shrink senses are tingling.

I'm worried about money, appropriately so given my income situation. I'm worried about not being able to speak French during this whole ordeal. Suppose I ask for a gas furnace and end up with a pink toilet instead? I'm worried about being able to focus on getting my new job up and running. And I'm worried about the state of the union, the marriage that is. Many a renovation has led to a house divided.

As inconvenient as it may be, there's no one else to blame for all this agitation. I made this decision and, as I recall, at the time I was legally an adult. One of these days I'll be grown up enough to realize that repeatedly choosing to live in a tornado has predictable side effects. But until then courage must be found and found *tout de suite*. Today is the first meeting at the Wreck with every *artisan* in Burgundy and by the end of it I know I will be dizzy. But I'm ready for this shit storm. The testosterone level will be in the red zone but I'm smack in the middle of PMS prime time. No wrecking balls required.

ROOTLESS TREE

I stole this title from one of my favourite Damien Rice songs that I'm listening to at top volume for a number of reasons. One, there's lots of swearing in the song so that suits me just fine right now. Two, I am soothed very much by music, so that's right on the money and three, I'm as tall as a tree and I can't find any roots to speak of. I'm moving. Again. Boxes and tape, hockey bags and a big white van. While I'm happy enough to move on to our more permanent residence (permanent being a relative term here), I am not digging this whole uprooting business. Etrochey has been so very kind to us and now I'm settled in with the cows and the chicken, lovingly referred to as Maxine, who has taken up permanent residence on our doorstep. I'm even making peace with the unknown creature that makes huge splashes in the river late at night.

I find it hard to believe that six weeks have gone by already. Yet in a way it seems like we've been here for an eternity. We've managed to leap over many bureaucratic hurdles and somehow I've managed to get roped into buying a house here. I can hardly remember my house in Canada. At the same time it seems like we just got here and I'm wondering how we've managed to spread our tentacles out into every room of this vast country house. I thought we'd brought very little with us but I appear to be wrong (a rare event).

I've moved too many times in my life and it's wearing me down. Even now I know that this next place is just a stopover until The Wreck is finished, likely in April (only with divine intervention will that house be done in April) and then I'm at it all over again. The good news is that I stayed in this next house while on vacation last year so at least I know what I'm getting.

So I say now with conviction, I am never moving again. No more will I taste the bitter packing tape as I rip it with my teeth because I've already packed every sharp object I own. No longer will I spend hours frantically trying to find the box that has the dental floss in it after eating a full rack of ribs at two in the morning. Never again shall I frighten the bejesus out of a sleeping husband by walking on sheets of bubble wrap on the four a.m. tinkle run. *Non, nein, nyet.* No one can make me. All right, one more time in April but after that no more. Once again I'm making plans and all I can hear is god laughing her ass off.

NOVEMBER

THE VIEW FROM HERE

In spite of all my ranting about moving we were set up in the new digs in no time, another splendid house brought to me by the miracle of discounted winter rental rates. A man from Paris and his American wife, who illustrates children's books at the table where I now sit, have lovingly transformed this little cottage into something truly marvelous. It boggles my mind as to how long it must have taken to put this place together. Nothing here, from the reclaimed painted floor tiles to the art nouveau armoires with their secret compartments, has been left to chance. Many years ago it was a functioning mill and the *Armançon* River runs literally right under the house, but I try not to think about that much. Everywhere I look there is something so Frenchy fine that I have to play Edith Piaf music all day just to complete the scene.

Every time I discover yet another wonder here I have to give my head a shake to remember that, for now, this is where I live, that there's no Monday morning at the hospital looming over my head and that makes everything, even moving, worthwhile.

HELLO, GOODBYE

The French are professional protesters and take great pride in their ability to chant and march in the streets against the issue *du jour*. And their skill in organizing massive walkouts (as we saw when we first arrived) is matched only by that of the Italians. But amid all the disobedience there is plenty of civility to be found.

Everyone knows about the kiss-kiss greetings here but what I didn't realize was how important greetings in general are to the French. A benefit of living here is that I can now see all kinds of things that I didn't while on vacation. Lately I'm taken by the custom of being greeted with a sing-song, *"Bonjour, Monsieur, Madame"* whenever we walk in somewhere, then when we leave the obvious, *"Au revoir, Monsieur, Madame."* I didn't really think much of it until I went to a local doctor's office for a flu shot. The waiting room door was closed and when I opened it I almost had a heart attack when everyone in the room sang out, *"Bonjour, Madame"* in unison. Then each time someone left to go into the doctor's office they were sent off with a cheery, *"Au revoir."* So I started paying close attention to this and sure enough, the same thing happens at the bank, the bakery, the stores, everywhere. It is a firm practice here and not once have I ever seen anyone enter or leave a place of business without offering an acknowledgment to everyone.

I know it doesn't sound like much but just imagine yourself walking into the Department of Motor Vehicles and singing out, "Hello, ladies and gentlemen," or leaving Tim Hortons with a hearty, "Goodbye, everyone, have a nice weekend." The place would be brought to a complete standstill with folks looking away uncomfortably and later laughing about the greeting fanatic they saw at the coffee shop that day. It's simply not done.

The French take many things seriously and salutations are no exception. Even when you clink glasses at the dinner table it's important to make eye contact as you say, *"Santé."* I've decided that I like it, a lot. I feel connected to people as soon as I walk in the door, like we're in this whole waiting for bread mess together. Why doesn't this happen in Canada I wonder? It's bizarre because Canada, Newfoundland in particular, is generally a very friendly culture. We're all in constant communication these days with our texting and twittering but we can't even say hello to one another while we wait for one of our most shared experiences—having our bodies repaired. I'm not saying that the French have managed to maintain a politesse that the rest of the world has abandoned. I'm just saying that it's lovely to have people say hello and wish you well on a regular basis.

I think everyone should give it a go at least once. At your next checkup swing open the waiting room door, pause until you have everyone's undivided attention and proudly call out, "Good day to you all." I think it might be the only way to get doctors to do routine mental health screens.

PREJUDICE AND PRIDE

While all this fun in France has been unfolding, a middle-aged woman with enough letters after her name to make any mother proud has become a trainee. It seems like only yesterday I made big decisions and used big words like serotonin reuptake inhibitor. I carried a pager that went off with annoying regularity at three in the morning. But today all I had to worry about was whether the fridge smelled like a bucket of stinky French *fromage* or if the towels looked better folded neatly on the bed or the dresser.

Yes, my long anticipated second career in vacation property management has begun. Over the past few weeks I've been job shadowing, otherwise known as working solely for the benefit of learning as I can't legally be paid in France yet. I've had the distinct privilege of scrubbing toilets, laundering linens, disposing of garbage, dusting and de-cobwebbing several charming stone cottages in the Burgundy countryside. According to my first on-the-job-training evaluation I'm the best rookie they've ever had. I'm the only one they've ever had and it was a self-evaluation, but that's beside the point.

It seems my obsessive need for cleanliness, once at the top of Neil's long list of Things That Annoy Me About My Wife, can now be officially moved to the special skills category on my CV. Is it the job of my dreams? Not on your life, but it is something worth doing. It may seem like I'm making fun of it but really I'm not. Sure, there wasn't a life and death situation to be found, but I did feel a peaceful satisfaction, a small degree of pride even, in making houses ready to receive the weary in need of a vacation, something I believe to be as important to life as breathing or dark chocolate. Like everything, it's all in how you see it. To me there's something noble about cleaning. I never understand why the janitors and hotel maids of this world never get the respect or the pay or even the thanks they deserve. Add in the newly transplanted immigrant factor and it's one of the toughest jobs out there. I certainly have a new regard for them.

Of course there is one more chore to be done—my mother. Specifically, how to help soften her transition from mother of a semi-fancy physician to that of a very un-fancy charwoman. Again, perhaps it's just a matter of perspective. Instead of mumbling, "The tall one ran away to France to scrub toilets," she could proudly say, "My elder daughter has decided to eschew the expected to pursue her dream abroad as an International Travel Facilitator."

For that matter, I suppose she could tell all her friends that I was the Canadian Cultural Attachée who has Sarkozy round for dinner twice a week. Who the hell would know the difference? I know for a fact that's what my grandmother, called Mamie (coincidentally the French word for grandma), would have said. I remember her parading me around St. Patrick's Mercy Home as The Doctor. I'm sure people thought that was actually my name. Every single time I went to visit her she'd tell everyone we saw that I was the best doctor in Canada who "ran" a big hospital in Halifax. This had the desired effect on all the other ladies who, as Mamie insisted, could never have produced such a clever grandchild. Who was I to contradict my elders?

Anyway, for now, I think this work suits me just fine. So far, the hardest part is deciphering the labels on the bottles of cleaners. After so much responsibility for so long, it's a tremendous relief to be concerned with small matters. The long-term plan for this venture is to become an extension of a not so small property rental and renovation business. But for the moment I'm at peace with my bucket and toilet brush and at the end of the day maybe that's all any mother or Mamie could ask for. That being said, I suspect that wherever my beloved late grandmother is (hopefully somewhere that has plenty of chocolate and Belvedere cigarettes) she's busy telling the tale of how I've taken up residence at the Palace of Versailles. If I happen to see her I'll be sure to let her know that I have a new job. I'll tell her I'm the President of France.

Oh the Humanity

I knew it was coming. Public humiliation. My French remains a vast wasteland dotted with the occasional noun, verb (present tense only) and adjective. To make matters worse, I finally met with my French teacher here in Semur only to find out that her daughter had just given birth in Sweden and my lessons would have to wait until the end of the month. Honestly, the nerve of some people. How can this baby, who probably already speaks perfect Swedish, take priority over me? Anyway, today I had the enviable experience of having to go to the pharmacy to get something desperately needed for a "lady" problem. I had two options, take Neil the translator with me and have him regale the pharmacist with a tale of my feminine woes or go it alone. I chose the latter, as the idea of having my husband in on this debacle seemed far too terrifying. It is my firm belief that the success of any marriage depends on judicious disclosure.

So off I went. As luck would have it, it happened to be about two o'clock and the pharmacy was packed after the two-hour lunch closure. I was wandering around desperately longing for the old days at Shoppers Drug Mart. I picked up some badly needed foot cream to stall the whole process when I heard the singsong call, "*Bonjour, Madame.*" There she was, a pretty young woman in a crisp white coat, sweet as *tarte tatin*, waiting to help me. I started with what I thought was much improved French, but I suddenly realized that I didn't really know any of the words I needed. This was not the time to fall back on my usual trick of gestures and jazz hands, pointing to the nether regions and such. She couldn't understand me so she called for the pharmacist to come help and I went through the whole thing again. Now, this was at a counter in the middle of the store with a large line of people behind me, all staring at the giant foreigner in their midst. I knew we were finally getting somewhere on the translation front when a lightbulb appeared to switch on in the young woman's head.

"Ah, *vaginale, vaginale!*" she exclaimed loudly, smiling at the pharmacist, obviously quite proud of herself for finally understanding me. Oh. My. Holy. Mother. You could've heard a pin drop in Siberia. Well, how wonderful. At least now everyone in Semur knows I have a vagina. This is exactly how I imagined being introduced to the locals.

But you can't keep a good vagina owner down. I regrouped and quickly started talking about the high cost of my items, trying to capitalize on my knowledge that the French don't exactly love to part with money. I could hear them murmuring their agreement and I hoped nobody noticed that my face was as red as a tomato and likely hot enough to fry an egg on. For god's sake, you're a doctor I thought; get a handle on yourself. Everyone was probably more disgusted by the crevice-filling heel cream than anything else that I was on about. On a positive note, I did manage to walk into a French pharmacy and walk out with what I needed, so I have to pat myself on the back for that. At the very least I'm prepared for the next feminine hygiene emergency. I'll just send Neil. I think the marriage can take it.

WHERE NOBODY
KNOWS YOUR NAME

Today I was meandering about town and I realized that I live in a place where absolutely no one knows me. This is a first for me. When I left St. John's some twelve years ago, I couldn't walk through the mall without running into half of my high school class. And in Halifax I had many friends and colleagues but here I'm an unknown, a nobody, an *étrangère*. Of course there's greatness to be found in anonymity. I can, if I want, run the full length of Rue de la Liberté wearing nothing but rubber boots and a wool toque singing *Oh Canada* top lung and no one would be able to identify me. I can go to the grocery store with varying degrees of bedhead and body odour and it doesn't really matter because there's no chance of running into a soul who knows me. I can even be humiliated beyond belief at the pharmacy and survive, simply because I am a foreign entity. Very liberating indeed. The thing is, I don't really want to run naked through the streets, at least not today. Liberated is one thing, isolated is another. Nobody knows me and maybe that's good. But that means I don't know anybody and that's not so good. The only folks I know live an hour away, not exactly convenient for a wine and whine session.

No Newfoundlander can live for very long without the art of the chat. We can squeeze a good two hours out of weather alone, and I am nothing if not defined by my excellent heritage. I need to know people. I also have a suspicion that I might, just might, be driving Neil bananas. At some point every couple runs out of things to talk about. My solution has been convincing him to let me post embarrassing pictures of him on the Internet, to which I know he has only agreed as a means of keeping me quiet for an hour. I assume socializing will come with time and with learning more French, but I can't wait that long. I need some English repartee and I need it now. There's a lady across the way who I see out walking her dog from time to time. Yesterday, I heard her speaking perfect English and it took everything I had not to run to her as fast as I could yelling, "DO YOU WANT TO PLAY WITH ME?" Instead, I've invited her over for a drink tomorrow night. Poor lady. I hope I don't frighten her to death with my pent-up chattiness, which I fear will gush out of my mouth like a raging river as soon as I open the door. It's like being a kid all over again, trying to make friends on the street and hoping you have at least one toy the other kids don't have, that one toy that elevates you from outcast to one of the gang. I don't have much in the way of toys but I do have that husband I could loan out for a night. He could use some time away from me.

LIFE ON THE
LOWER WEST SIDE

Many years ago when I was young and snappy, I had serious dreams of running away to New York City to become a theatre performer. I had no idea what kind of theatre would have me but I never doubted that I would end up there some day living in a hip apartment in a hip neighbourhood with hip friends. Now I suspect a broken hip is all I'd find if I began prancing about on a stage in the Big Apple. The point is, I always saw myself as a city gal. True, I've never lived in a major city for any length of time, but I've also never lived in a place with fewer than 150,000 people. I remember going from St. John's to Toronto as a kid and being infected with big city energy and fascinated by the masses of people of every colour and creed. But mostly I recall being whipped into a state of consumer frenzy by all the things you could buy beyond my small corner of the world. St. John's was always the last place in Canada to stock all the things we saw on cable TV channels piped in from exciting places in America like Bangor and Detroit.

So, this past weekend I embarked on my Get To Know Semur Excursion, and so far I've learned two things. One, I am the tallest woman in town and I'm thoroughly shocked by this. Oh, of course not. The second is that I have chosen to live in a town where I cannot purchase a cellphone. I already have one, I'm just saying that if I needed to buy one I'd have to drive to another town. Then again, this is all about seeking a simpler life, one that allows me to live on a very modest income. Obviously restricted access to shops and services helps in this regard, but that doesn't mean that I don't need time to adjust. I mean there's no Mac store here. What do I do if my computer breaks down? There's no video store, so losing myself in the latest indie flick for $4.99 isn't happening any time soon. At night there isn't a creature about, so midnight martinis and tapas are also things of the past. Today I had the first feelings of doubt about living somewhere so quiet and small. Now I'm not saying that there's nothing to be had here. I can walk two minutes up the road and find a stunning, 18th century armoire. It's more the everyday convenience type things that I've grown accustomed to that are nowhere to be found. I'm not sure I can do this. Of course, this would have been useful information to have before purchasing a house here. I'll have to adjust somehow.

I eventually did get to New York City but it wasn't until 2004 and the only performance I gave was that of an enraptured audience member of *La Bohème* at The Met. So for now, I must be content with living on the lower west side of Semur, the town that always sleeps. Instead of a view of the Hudson I have the River *Armançon* at my doorstep. And as for performing, you can catch me every day and every night playing the role of a woman who doesn't want anything more than she already has.

Champagne Taste, Beer Budget

So back to the Wreck of the Hesperus. We had our big meeting to review all the work estimates and as usual we have created a plan that only a Trump could love. What exactly is wrong with us? Perhaps we are fundamentally incapable of doing anything on a small scale. We started out with a very modest plan: an open living room, kitchen and eating area and two small rooms upstairs, a bedroom for us and an office for Neil. This has somehow ballooned into an addition out the back that juts out onto an enormous wall of rock and has the world's most complicated roof design. Plus two full bathrooms (to prevent divorce) as well as a half bathroom on the main floor because apparently I'm too lazy to go upstairs every 20 minutes (my bladder and a tea bag, same size), and a full revamping of the exterior.

Now the house has nothing, as in dirt floors nothing. These tremendously talented *artisans* cost money and we've already overpaid the Parisian *artiste* for *la maison* to begin with, so now it's down to some really tough decisions. We could overextend ourselves to finance the big plan and hope that our venture into the world of toilet cleaning pays off. We'd live happily ever after, sipping cheap wine on the terrace of the small but not so simple house. Or we could scale it right back to bare bones and turn it into a little vacation house that could possibly provide some income, very little income, so a gamble for sure. There is a third somewhat hideous option. We could decide that we simply cannot make a go of it and walk away despite being beyond the time permitted to do so. This would mean a pull-out penalty (Catholics, not a word) of over 9,000 euros, which is like a million dollars Canadian. Okay, it's actually more like $13,000, but it might as well be a million to me because to pay that for a French real estate lesson might send me right round the friggin' pipe.

So, for the next few days we'll be frantically reviewing and discussing all the relevant details to try and come to a decision about what to do. And, *comme d'habitude*, as the stress level rises, I take to thinking and talking to myself. On the one hand I say, what the hell? I came for the big game action, so I can motor on and the worst that happens is I'd have to sell it. But steady on old girl, houses take a really long time to sell here so this could be big trouble, as in financial ruin. Okay, then do it up as a rental and there's a possibility for some income and investment reward. Hang on now my friend. After you dump money into the reno, you then have to buy furniture and linens, fully stock a kitchen, and provide all the other bells and whistles that make a successful vacation property. Then where will the money be found for a place for you and Big Red to live? Does anyone else talk to themselves like this?

I have no idea where this is going. The next couple of days will be difficult and I can't help thinking that all this crap reminds me of something. What is it I wonder? Oh yes, my old life, the one I moved heaven and Earth to escape from. As my mother always says, you can't run away from your feet.

THE EAST VILLAGE

Many discoveries have been made by venturing away from the funky French cottage here on the lower west side, all the way to the opposite side of town, which carries a grand commute of about, oh I'd say, twelve minutes. Walking. Granted a short distance by city standards, but it does require a quadriceps-burning ascent up a set of stone stairs that, for the time being, fortuitously eliminates the need for spin classes and StairMasters. By the time I get to town I'm a sweating, panting mess of a woman. At least I've found a way to counteract all my *croissant* gorging. So, throughout the grey and rainy days of late I've been traipsing about what I call the east village. Sadly, my dreams of catching Patti Smith and Sam Shepard lounging at the café have not materialized, but all is not lost. I found a large organic food shop and a very charming lingerie boutique, so herb teas and breasts are covered.

What I've also discovered is that my east village, just like the one of my teenage dreams, is home to artists and rockers alike. I managed to find an art and antique shop that is currently showing some edgy graphic prints as well as some funky antique jewelry and the most beautiful collection of Christmas ornaments I've ever seen. As for the rock element, well, I did see a guy outside the *tabac* wearing a leather headband and a white tank top in the cold November rain. I'm assuming that he left his coat at home in order to display his dog collar and the collection of spiked armbands that ran the full length of both arms. So maybe he's no Iggy Pop, but he's what I've got. Add to the mix the discovery of a small theatre promising a performance by one of the finest pianists in France next month and the hipster scene is complete.

Yes, this town is more than I gave it credit for, I think. It's no mecca of the urbane but it's still a charming town in one of the most beautiful regions of France and offers the allure of a foreign culture. All that's missing now is my usual gang of chic gay boyfriends. How I miss my Canadian boys like Colin whose comment on my new grey hair was, "Girl, your eyes are piercing." Really, how can I be expected to live without this sort of thing? I've heard that Semur actually has a gay community and finding that will be my next project. Or I can just sit and wait for it to find me, which always happens no matter where I wander.

My very clever sister says she imagines my life must be like living in a French film—despair, chaos and drama surrounded by impossibly chic knickknacks. Well, on my lower west side, the chaos, drama and knick-knacks are here and the despair is only occasional. All that's missing now in my east village is a Mapplethorpe exhibit and a man to help me dress for it.

CHEZ SERGE

Now I imagine very few people come here to see Christmas baubles. I'd say whenever people think about France the first two things that come to mind are food and wine. There are several big grocery stores in town and I was surprised to discover that the *Intermarché* is remarkably similar to any Canadian grocery store I've been to, well, apart from all the labels that I can't read and a meat counter that sells rabbits with their heads still attached. But one of my favourite things found in France is the *épicerie*, a small boutique food store. When I first visited Paris I fell in love with one in Montmartre, not just for the food but also for the unmistakable Frenchiness of the store itself. I thought that such gastronomic luxury would be limited to larger cities, but right here in this tiny town is a store that rivals any Parisian gourmet boutique. On the sidewalk, under the cherry red awning, there are stalls with everything from fresh oysters on ice to exotic mushrooms. And when you walk through the red door, it takes you in body and soul, and transports you to another time. It's one of the most thoughtfully considered food shops I've ever seen.

The styling of the cans is almost enough to make me eat sardines. Of course you pay a little extra for all these delicacies, but browsing is free as is a chat with Serge, who tells me that I look a lot like his wife. Obviously a man of impeccable taste. At least I have an angle for a discount on that bottle of Volnay in the back.

FATHER FORGIVE ME
FOR I HAVE SINNED

Perhaps a tad dramatic as I have not committed a mortal sin, at least not yet today. But I do have a confession to make and, as a recovered Catholic, I have no idea how else to begin. Many a time I knelt in the dark of the confessional, ready to be absolved for the transgressions committed that week. Whatever crime against humanity I'd masterminded over at Pius X Girl's School had to be put forth to avoid the fires of hell. At least it was always confidential and anonymous. Why else would you be protected from the long line of sinners outside by a threadbare velvet curtain and obscured from the priest by a high tech square of wire screen? Although, I must admit I had my doubts when my sessions would end with Father Ken saying, "Say ten Hail Marys and tell your mother I'll be up for supper Friday night."

Anyway, my most recent deep and dark is that despite being in the land of haute cuisine, and indeed the food here is nothing short of miraculous, there are foods that I find I'm missing. It's a shameful list and borders on the ridiculous, but then again so does my whole life these days. I've previously mentioned my longing for sour cream, and all those people who say *crème fraîche* is just as good should be on their knees because lying is a sin.

No sour cream anywhere but also no ginger ale in a can, no Miracle Whip or Monterey Jack cheese. No President's Choice lemonade. No ribeye steaks and no fresh guacamole or salsa, and as for making my own, I'm way too inept for such endeavours. No honey garlic spare ribs or wonton soup. No marble rye, no pastrami, no French's Mustard, so no sandwich. It's a sad list when you live in a place where Meursault wine is made half an hour down the road and *foie gras* practically falls from the sky. I really do want to eat fresh, local food and for the most part that's what I've been doing. But I still long for all the things that once had a regular spot on the grocery list. Even though the stores here are bursting with gastronomic wonders, I really miss my crappy foodstuff because it's just part of what I knew day in and day out, all part of the everything left behind.

So there, I've said it. I live in France and I'm dying for some Miracle Whip. Let's take me out back and beat the *merde* out of me. Instead, I'll confess my sins. There's a spectacular church up in town and I'm polishing up my Act of Contrition and tearing up the house looking for a set of rosary beads. I can't imagine what the penance here is for pining for fake mayonnaise, so I think it might be best to keep my plans to open up a Gap and a Blockbuster to myself.

SHOW ME
THE MONEY

Removing every hair on my lower body one at a time with
rusty tweezers.

Watching every Steven Seagal and Jean-Claude Van Damme movie
ever made back to back for 48 hours straight.

Flying from France to Australia the morning after being crowned
champion at an international hot wing eating/tequila shooter contest.

Attending a three-day conference on the mating habits of the
South American carpenter ant.

Anything that goes on behind the closed door of a
gynecologist's office.

Having the Newfoundland flag tattooed across my tongue.

Untangling 27 sets of Christmas lights.

Quantum physics.

Working as Celine Dion's personal assistant.

Trying on bathing suits in early March under fluorescent lighting.

Things that are all way easier, way more fun and way less painful than getting a renovation mortgage in France.

DECEMBER

MEMBERSHIP
HAS ITS PRIVILEGES

I was having one of those days, a day when the moments of weakness far outnumber the moments of fortitude, and I started thinking about getting on the first Air Canada jet bound for the homeland. When you have nothing better to do, it's easy to find time to let the trials and tribulations of living in a foreign country overwhelm your kind and gentle nature. It started with the fact that we cannot find snow tires for our little French car, known affectionately as the blue bubble. Here in the land of Michelin, not a tire to be found. How is it possible that the world's biggest tire factory is practically right down the road but we can't get winter tires? I found this out after returning from the now famous pharmacy where I was trying to find a between the knee pillow necessary for all those with spines of glass. Of course I had to deal with *Mademoiselle Vaginale*, an added bonus. The trouble is, because I didn't understand a bloody word she said, I left unsure of whether I ordered the pillow or not. My nerves are just about gone.

Then I discovered these mysterious red lesions that have been popping up all over my body. The glamour never ends over here. I couldn't call to get a doctor's appointment because phone French is beyond me. So, I threw on a bit of lipstick to try and look presentable and raced up to town to get to the local GP's office before the big lunchtime shutdown. I walked into the clinic only to see a notice on the waiting room wall that said the only female doctor in the area was not taking any new patients. Oh, I see. Fine.

I whipped off my coat, started beating the floor with it, while shrieking, "OF COURSE SHE'S NOT TAKING NEW PATIENTS! SOMEONE GET ME A BUCKET OF WINE RIGHT NOW! I DON'T CARE THAT IT'S ONLY 11:30. IT'S FRANCE AND YOU ALL DRINK WINE FOR BREAKFAST IN THIS GODFORSAKEN WASTELAND OF A COUNTRY SO SHUT UP!" Then I picked up a chair and hurled it through the large plate glass window.

No, not really. I haven't completely succumbed to my inner toddler yet, but I will say that I was frustrated enough to let this scenario play out in my head a little longer than I should have. Instead, I waited for all the patients to be seen, and when the doctor came out my redheaded interpreter and I pounced on her. She took us into her office and we explained our situation. To my complete amazement she said that we could negotiate, maybe she could agree to take on one or two new people here and there. I was waiting for the part where I had to offer Neil's services for Saturday nights (by this I mean cooking and fixing stuff), but in the end she just asked about our health and offered to examine me right then and there. On the one hand this was marvelous. On the other hand, when I took my coat off I was shocked to see that I was still wearing the frayed Tabasco Hot Sauce T-shirt I had slept in. I was particularly thrilled to see that the big blob of dark chocolate smeared on the front of it had somehow survived the night. Again, it's one big issue of Paris Vogue after another with me.

Anyway, she was entirely gracious, gave me a referral to a dermatologist, checked the rest of me over and then didn't charge me for the appointment because I was a colleague. I knew that all those years of school and a six-figure student loan would be worth it someday. If only I'd been a mechanic. I would've had my tires yesterday.

Social Papillon

Say what you will about the perils of modern technology, but I'd be lost without it. If not for Skype, email and internet telephone lines, I'd have bailed out long ago. I've been chatting with lots of friends from home lately and I actually feel social again, even if it is only in the virtual sense. In reality, I've been quite the socialite this past weekend. On Saturday night we braved the arctic weather for an evening at the *Café Des Arts*. They were hosting an exhibition for a Parisian artist who was in attendance, wearing cowboy boots, a biker jacket and tight red jeans, a perfectly appropriate ensemble for a man in his 60s. There was also another fancy gentleman, silk cravat and all, referred to as Maestro. Maestro of what I don't know — perhaps a famous European symphony, although my guess is he's the local high school music teacher who insists that everyone call him that. Some days my life seems far too inspired by *Seinfeld*.

On Sunday we were doubly blessed. My neighbour, Elizabeth, who has taken me on as a bit of a project, took us for a fantastic lunch at the home of her friends, Anne and Michel. We feasted on Swiss sausage cooked in wine while admiring their stunning French farmhouse. We lingered for hours at their dining table — an enormous slab of wood suspended from the ceiling by huge chains opposite an ancient fireplace big enough to stand in. The walls were lined from floor to ceiling with books, and from my chair I could see the *atelier* outside where Anne crafts gorgeous silver jewelry. They offered us the use of their apartment in Switzerland (not much to think about on that one) and we marveled at their kindness to two souls lost in the heart of Burgundy. Later in the day, Michel and Patricia came for a visit. We poked around at the Wreck and caught up on the news from Etrochey, and it was wonderful to see them again.

Relief, or as the French say *soulagement*, was the word of the day. Interesting things to do, new friends and a break from being the Village Idiot. I was very well-behaved, not one embarrassing episode all weekend. Perhaps the madness is settling and I will now have a normal, boring but Frenchy cool life. Somehow I'll learn to speak French, I'll be socially successful and the house will come together smoothly. Maybe all the humiliation and weirdness is behind me. Of course, tomorrow is another day and as I skip and twirl over the Pont Pinard singing, "The hills are alive," I know the universe is plotting its revenge.

THE BIG CHILL

Hey Canada, I found your winter here in France. Come get it. It's so cold here Brigitte Bardot is wearing a sealskin coat. Ice and snow have brought most of the UK and France to a slow crawl. Thousands of flights have been cancelled and trucks, the lifeline of Europe, have been stranded for days, which means that every delay in France now has an excuse — the weather. Next the bank will be telling me that the mortgage approval is still not ready because of the weather and my head might actually explode. Here in Semur, we've not seen the sun for over a month now and I'm just waiting for rickets to set in. Maybe I thought France would be warmer and sunnier, but I'm not complaining. Other parts of the country have been really dumped on and, compared to a Newfoundland winter, this place is practically tropical.

But then, I come from the land of professional winter survivors. We really know how to handle it with plows and salt and such. Here they just look frightened and descend into panic mode. I'm stunned by the amount of snow that creates havoc over here. Fifteen centimetres? Sure that's a mere dusting, nothing that can't be managed with a slight eye roll and the latest snazzy scraper from Canadian Tire. I'm not buying this whole surprised by winter business. Scientists the world over have confirmed that winter comes every year and at about the same time. But I have to go a little easy on the French, as apparently this kind of weather almost never occurs before January. And it might be our fault. Everywhere we go I can see the locals looking at us and putting *deux* and *deux* together. An early winter coincides with the arrival of two Canadians who appear to have multiple down coats and several wooly hats apiece. I admit it does look a bit suspicious.

But at least I know how to dress for winter. The other day I was walking in town wearing my full-length shearling coat, a trapper hat and of course my non-slip Timberland boots. Why, in my view, I could have just slipped unnoticed into the crowd at the Sundance Film Festival. Then I saw her coming out of the flower shop, a lovely little grey beret and trendy cinched-waist coat, an artfully draped silk scarf and high-heeled boots. Ah yes: me,

Nanook of the North. Her, Ice Queen of Europe. At least she'll look gorgeous as she's going down on that icy cobblestone. I'm just thankful she can't see me at home in my long johns, wool socks and fleece slippers. Stone cottages are quaint, but warm they ain't.

So I'm settling in for the long haul here. The wine will flow, the bakeries will keep pumping out *croissants* and the grocery stores now have entire aisles devoted to Christmas chocolates. Like every year, I'll tough it out until spring. Someone wake me when it's April.

DECISIONS, DECISIONS

Wreckgate continues. The deadline for financing has come and gone and the initial answer from the bank was, " we might consider financing your lovely *maison* … with just a few conditions." A few conditions they said, like get French life insurance because we don't accept that silly Canadian insurance that you've had for ten years. And we don't feel like financing your kitchen because your range, fridge and clever Ikea cabinets and countertops are "portable." And if any unexpected costs crop up during the renovation, you're on your own with that. So *bon courage* and we appreciate your business.

Well, how interesting. For a number of reasons I find those terms entirely unacceptable. I'm old and decrepit, literally falling apart at the seams and Neil takes medication with an annual cost equal to that of a Mercedes, so applying for new life insurance is not an optimistic undertaking, no pun intended. And this portable concept is confusing to me. What do they think I'm going to do? Rip off the countertops and strap them to my back on the next Air Canada flight? As for unexpected costs, I've done enough renovations to know that it would not be unusual to find out, mid-project, that the house is built on an ancient burial ground requiring a team of voodoo priests to sign off on it to the tune of $25,000. Banks, gotta love 'em. To think it only took them two months to come up with this brilliant response. So for the first time in the whole mortgage-o-rama, these conditions create an opportunity for us to walk away penalty free. Of course then what? As of May 1st, we're homeless. There are slim pickings for rental opportunities here in Semur, except for vacation houses that I couldn't afford now for a week let alone for months at a time.

In the meantime, as if this isn't complicated enough, we'll begin talks with a second bank, which means another month or so of deliberations over the proposed project and, come May 1st, we're still homeless. We could look for another house that needs less work, but there's not much to choose from. I have no idea what to do. So, as my mother and her mother before her always said, there's nothing to do but to "offer it up." Good advice. I'll reflect and pray, meditate and intoxicate and see what comes of it. Mostly I'd like to offer it right up *Monsieur* Bank's arse.

MIDDLE-AGE SPREAD

In the meantime, my midsection is in love with France and it has decided to show its affection by expanding exponentially. I'm gone right doughy (translation: I have become unusually soft and squishy). No wonder—I've never eaten so much bread and pastry in my life. I've always been skinny, so this being shaped like a sausage is something new. About two weeks ago, I buttoned my comfy, mannish Levis and there it was, a jellyroll, the proverbial muffin top. I went through the whole mess of excuses. Demonic French laundry machines shrinking my pants, temporary bloating from the change in diet, retaining water from something connected to the joys of womanhood, and I was pleased particularly because I saw no reason to deviate from my daily carbohydrate festival. Except that a week later, the muffin top was now one of those super size ones sold by the case at Costco along with barrels of olive oil and laundry detergent. Maybe this was somehow related to my eating habits.

Still, my denial was in full force until yesterday. I had eaten half a box of chocolates, part of a large chocolate horse filled with gooey caramel (a Semur specialty), a *pain au chocolat*, a gigantic Nutella and banana sandwich and for dinner, veal scaloppini with mash and veg. Then I enjoyed some corn chips, dark chocolate and a fruity soda called Agrum while watching a movie. I can't remember what I had for breakfast and lunch, but I know I had something. I was lying on my side in bed, mystified by the crampy stomach I was suffering from. My lovely husband lay down behind me to give me a cuddle, which he was obliged to do because I was whining like a two-year-old about retaining water. He put his hand on my stomach in a there-there gesture and this is what I heard from the man behind me, "What's that?" Then this is what the man behind me did. He took the protruding flesh in his hand, started jiggling it, and said, "What's that?" clearly finding himself enormously funny.

Well, there it is. Oh, we laugh about it now. Or at least I pretend to laugh. I guess I should be grateful to him for breaking through my web of defenses, and I am. So grateful that I think I'll return the favour. The next time we're in public, I'll grab something that protrudes from his body, jiggle it and say, "What's that?" A good marriage is all about the give and take. I know he'll thank me for it later.

The First Noël

With all that's been going on lately, I've completely forgotten that it's almost Christmas. Of course I don't really do Christmas. As a childfree woman, I've usually been on call, and since it's often the busiest time of year in psychiatry, it's always been something I hoped would come and go quickly. Also, due to our constant renovating, Neil and I have gradually gotten out of the present thing. He gives me a toilet, I give him a bag of tile grout and we call it a day. In fact, over the last few years I've managed to almost entirely extricate myself from the yearly tumult. Now, watching it from afar, it looks quite ridiculous and always makes me scratch my head. Two people plan to give each other and their families gifts for Christmas. This involves fighting over parking spaces, racing through malls, sweating with screaming kids in the lines at Wal-Mart, racking up credit cards to buy things that nobody really needs, followed by three days in bed and a year of payments to recover from the joy of it. Why don't people just pay each other's light bill and go have a few drinks together? I'm no humbug. I love the idea of Christmas, I just don't understand the madness it's become. We all know there's not a whole lot of peace and goodwill going on at Future Shop on the 24th of December.

This first French Christmas will obviously be different for us. We don't have any ornaments so we'll skip the tree. On Christmas Eve we're meet-

ing with the second bank to see if they will give us a mortgage that actually allows for a kitchen. And for a change, this year we gave each other something other than drywall dust—a ticket. Jean-Philippe Collard, a renowned French pianist, has friends here in Semur and a couple of times a year he comes and plays in the tiny medieval theatre. So last night we ventured out with Semur's finest citizens as well as people who came from Switzerland just to hear him play in such a small venue.

Despite being delayed by winter weather, he arrived and sat at the Steinway without a moment of practice and gave a breathtaking performance as a rather large bat flew wildly about the theatre. Yes, of course there was a bat. In between pieces, this elegant man (think silver-haired Alan Rickman) stood and talked about the composers, their music and who knows what else. I didn't have to know what he was saying because it was enough just to take in the spectacle. Our neighbour Elizabeth, a classically trained pianist herself, was as proud to present him to us as if he were her own creation. It was a magical night and for me, this is what Christmas is all about—being with someone you love, doing something you enjoy, experiencing something that makes your heart glad and your soul soften. Well, that and a big load of fancy French chocolates.

Baptism by Fire

This chapter will be written in perfect literary French. Oh, how I wish I weren't lying. I couldn't write much more than, "I'd like a glass of white wine please," but there's something to be said for this whole immersion idea. Between my lessons, French television and living here, I'm happy to say that I understand a fair bit more than when I arrived. It's a back and forth thing though, as just when I think I'm doing fine, someone comes along speaking *très vite* and I'm lost all over again. Well, I'd better get it together because pretty soon Neil heads back to the land of sour cream and Shoppers Drug Mart for seven whole days. Something to do with that stuff he does to pay for everything.

He's leaving me here, alone in a foreign country where I am perfectly capable of ordering a complete meal but totally incapable of communicating in an emergency, like, "I've accidentally cut my hand off trying to make something called dinner." I mean there's just so much that could go wrong. Number one, I may actually starve to death. All right, that's a bit over the top, but seven days of grilled cheese sandwiches and chocolates can't be good for you. Plus, I believe I mentioned that river that runs under

our house. Last week it was so high that it flooded over the road and the little wall that surrounds our happy *maison*. It took Neil half a day to talk me down from the ceiling. Finally, the intricate plumbing of this cottage completely freaks me out. The sewage gets pumped from the house, as does the other water, by some crafty system located in the cave under the house. It's so finicky that only one plumber in the area knows how to deal with it. Just the other day the grey water pump seized up and flooded the bathroom. I was standing there washing my hands, preoccupied with examining the canyon developing between my eyebrows, when suddenly I was up to my ankles in water. Only after determining that it was water from the sink and dishwasher did I resume breathing. Neil had to descend into the dark watery cave through a trap door in the floor and do something that disconnected the pump. Now the water just splashes into the cave until the plumber can come next week.

What in the name of all that is holy am I doing with that mess when he's gone? I've heard stories about black water back-ups in the past, and let me be perfectly clear: if that sewage pump fails it's all over. I shall have to go down with the ship because there's no way that cave and I are coming face to face. Anyway, there's not a moment to lose. I have to spend the next few weeks learning every phrase connected to every kind of disaster I can think of. First on the list: "Excuse me kind sir, there seems to be a river of sewage in my kitchen. Can you please send a biohazard team, and while you're at it perhaps a nice pot of *coq au vin*?"

January

Ring Out
the Old

Another shiny new year. I suppose I should take a moment to reflect over the past year as the new one begins. And I would, if only I knew where to start. It's not every year I leave behind a life that took 42 years to build, toss all reason out the window and set up a situation like the one I've got going on here. I started to make a list of all the things that have happened and I stopped halfway through because I was exhausted. Let's just say 2010 has been somewhat eventful. Looking back on it now, it's hard to put together how it all came about. One day I was sitting in the rounds room in a Canadian hospital and the next I was living in a medieval French town and cutting my own hair with an electric razor. It all happened so fast and now seems so far away, nothing more than a blur.

Today as I walked past the Wreck, I realized that I couldn't even remember everything I sold or gave away; all the unnecessary things that always seemed so important to have. Even now I know I have a few things packed away in boxes here but I couldn't say exactly what. I hardly recognize myself anymore, a small town, silver-haired woman who eats pastry around the clock and asks her husband for money. There's really no way to fully describe the impact of so much change at once. But I have to give myself credit, I've survived until this point. Three and a half months in, a bit banged up but still standing. I admit there are days when I think I've made a wrong turn but that's only here and there, mostly at the pharmacy. All jokes aside, it hasn't been easy but it has been interesting.

I have no idea what this next year will bring, and that's a good thing. If someone had told me last year what 2010 was about to bring, I would have been compelled to write them a prescription. The only thing I ask for is the ability to roll with it as it comes. I imagine if this year is anything like the last, I might need to be sedated. So I say to 2010, thank you for bringing me here and for carrying me this far. And to 2011, I say bring it on ya tricky bastard. I can take whatever you've got. Wrecks, toilets, verb conjugation meltdowns, raging rivers, expanding waistlines, a plague of locusts, you name the time and place and I'll show up. I'm sticking with The Big

French Adventure, no matter what. Fate, Destiny, did you hear what I said? Maybe if you aren't too busy you can ask Lady Luck to stop by and see me.

WRECK-O-RAMA

Wreck-o-drama is more like it. *Monsieur* Bank has given his final word, a clearly enunciated, "*Non.*" In the end, they refused to finance our project as requested because it was considered too much of a risk. Anyone with eyes can see that I'm a risk in general but still, I can't help but feel insult-ed. The rejection was based on a report by an independent evaluator sent from Dijon who took one look at the Wreck and politely requested that the Canadians kiss his *derrière*. The realtor, the property company folks and my neighbour, who's been in Semur for over 30 years, all said they'd never seen this kind of evaluation done in France. Of course not. I move to France and all kinds of bizarre things come out of the woodwork: the coldest December in 40 years, the least amount of sunshine in 20 odd years and now novel methods of real estate obstruction. Coincidence? I think not.

But it's not all gloomy. As with almost every disappointment, there is a very sparkly silver lining here. After the slap from *la banque* we went back to our plans for the reno and discovered they were off everywhere by about two feet. Had we been given the go ahead we would've had a huge problem on our hands. The bottom line is the deal is dead, for now.

Undaunted, we went back to the drawing table, literally, and spent every minute of the holidays reworking the design. The challenge here is for me, a giant North American, to live and work in 800 square feet with a husband without committing a homicide. I think we've finally arrived at a plan that preserves life, so now we have to start the whole process over from scratch. We have yet to meet with the second bank as the weather on Christmas Eve made country back road travel a death wish. To proceed with this new application we have to get all new quotes from the *artisans*, which will take weeks and weeks. All this is assuming that the Wreck will still be available and the lady from Paris will be willing to deal with us again.

One of the many good things about France is that you can't throw a rock without hitting a wreck. This week we are looking at more wrecks, continuing the quest for the original Wreck, as well as trying to figure out where the hell we'll live in May if we don't have a house by then. But the secret is that throughout this whole process something has not quite fit for me; something's not right. For the first time in the ten years I've spent on a hobby that has come to feel like a second career, I found the whole design process tedious and even irritating. I resented having to spend any of my time on it. In between pastries I'll have to take a long look at that one.

Ah yes, the simple life. Freedom from commotion and complications. The quiet laid back pace that I've been seeking. As I've said before, it's a sickness. Real Estateitis, Renovationosis, Wreckemia, more commonly known as same *merde*, different country.

Skin Deep

But let me say more about those red lesions all over my body. The ignore-and-hope-they- go-away strategy was surprisingly unsuccessful, so a trip to the dermatologist was inevitable. She's right here in town with a very impressive setup I must say—a swanky office in her equally swanky house.

I decided the way to go on this one was *sans* husband as translator because no matter how gentle her lighting scheme is, there's no fun in having your better two-thirds watch an all over body surveillance from the sidelines. I told her I didn't speak French very well. *"Pas de problème,"* she said and launched into the *parlez-vous* with alarming speed. Not that it mattered. There are only two dermatological outcomes, cream or cutting. So, when I heard a word that sounded like eczema, I knew which way it was going. As it turns out, the highly mineralized water, which leaves a thick white film over everything it touches, also causes many a foreigner to require her services. Well, she's a genius, this one. The scaly red welts are almost gone thanks to cream number one and instead of looking like an alligator, I now resemble an oil slick, thanks to cream number two. Well worth the 66 euros that this little adventure set me—rather, the bread-earning husband—back.

And speaking of skin, scales and being set back a few bucks, I can't help but notice that my perfect face cream, found after a decade of trial and error, is down to the wire. Crème de la Mer has long been my only beauty indulgence and, at over two hundred bucks a jar, I'm pretty sure this one is my last. This is one frill for which I simply cannot ask my *Monsieur* to fork over the dough. I have always treated myself to it because I've never been a mani/pedi kind of gal, although I did have something waxed once. I figured one lady luxury still kept me in the low maintenance category. Not that I couldn't benefit from a spa day. My hands say farming and my feet are too disgusting to even talk about. Perhaps I'll embrace the bio-chic trend and start making my own cream with olive oil and river water. I am joking, of course, buttering bread is a chore for me. It's likely that the million-dollar *crème* is nothing more than Vaseline with a shot of algae, but I'll still miss it.

The good news is that I did manage to catch that the dermatologist here does facial fillers. *Vive la France*. No Chinese food or video stores, but you can get your lips done up Mrs. Pitt perfect. My face will be flaking off but I'll able to lick my lips and stick myself to the windshield. I just know Big Red would be happy to pay a couple of hundred clams to see that one.

Dollars and Sense

People often ask me for advice about how to set fire to the cubicle and walk away from a fully formed life. The truth is, I don't have a good answer. This is no how-to manual, simply the tale of one woman's attempt to live a different life with no promise of a happy ending. To be sure my situation is unique; no kids, an EU passport and a ready and willing Rusty the Wonder Husband, all of which make this easier for me than it would be for most. But one thing I've learned is that transforming a life lived into a life wanted has a lot to do with money; specifically, finding a way to live without it.

I don't have any debt but only because I worked like a dog for 15 years to pay back the loan that bought me the stack of diplomas that are now collecting dust in my mother-in-law's basement. While I don't have a big wad of cash, I do have the proceeds from the sale of my house and everything that was in it. However, this won't go far in France. Apparently, I've landed in the town with the most expensive houses in Burgundy. Of course I have. Anywhere else would have been downright sensible and that, it seems, is not how I roll. The secret so far is simply to spend less. Since September I have purchased French lessons, a portable player for language CDs, a sweater, a cure for red lesions, hair gel and, my big splurge, a few books for my Kindle. The only other expenses I have are insurance policies and one charity that I support monthly. Neil, god love him, pays for food, lodging and tampons.

But the real trick is not to just to spend less, but to want less, and it's not easy. I'm the kind of person who doesn't want anything as long as I stay home. I never know I want grey suede boots until I see them walking past me on the feet of an impossibly chic French woman. I thought I'd be safe here in such a small town, and I was until I stumbled upon Amazon

France. Oh very dangerous territory this. I now have access to everything like European boots, shoes and bags (freezing the credit card may be the only strategy here) and English books (burn the credit card), all with free delivery right to my river step. Now that I can actually get anything I want, I want one of everything. I'm pretty sure I don't really need a gold sequined clutch purse, but that doesn't change the fact that it could be here in three days, delivered by the post lady who speeds along the river on a bright yellow bicycle. Oh, sweet seduction. My rambling point is that this journey is all about tradeoffs. To make this work, I have to be willing to give up what I occasionally get duped into thinking I want. I just need to remember that Amazon doesn't sell the experience of a lifetime and that's what it's all about. Words to live by I'm sure, but I just know that a tiara and black motorcycle boots would add a certain *je ne sais quoi* to the whole operation.

THE COMPANY
OF STRANGERS

Here in Semur, under the 16th century *Porte Guillier*, there is an inscription: *Les Semurois Se Plaisent Font En L'Acointance Des Estrangeres*. Translated it means that the people of Semur take pleasure in meeting strangers. Since 1552. As far as I can tell they take it very seriously and they're remarkably good at it. After over 400 years of practice, this shouldn't come as a surprise. Before moving here, I was concerned about how we would be received and perceived. Maybe *les Semurois* would see us as boorish North American invaders rolling into town with big plans to buy up their land and erect a Wal-Mart. I was fearful of becoming local pariahs, shunned and isolated. I'd be forced to wander aimlessly through the streets in a tattered pink chenille bathrobe, randomly conjugating verbs and begging someone to have tea with me.

It's still early, but for the moment I think I can hold off on the woman-on-the-edge routine. We've been making small inroads into the Semur scene. We attended the annual town meeting where the mayor greeted us with style. The man bowed and kissed my hand, which is how I've decided all men should now receive me. We've even done some hosting ourselves.

Neil served his very French *lapin au vin* to my French teacher Patricia and her friend Francis. We've been introduced to the *très elegante* Jacqueline, owner of the lingerie store who may convince me that bra shopping is not torture. And we've been invited to a dinner party where *Monsieur* Mayor himself will be in attendance. Word of the Canadian invasion is spreading.

Whenever the townspeople ask us why we moved here, and they all ask, we rattle off the many things we like about Semur and they all seem so pleased that their town has somehow spoken to us. When we tell them how welcoming everyone has been they smile knowingly. "Of course," they say, "this is our history." That's all fine for now, but once I start speaking French well enough for my foot to find its way back to my mouth, all bets will be off. History or no history, I know that robe is coming out.

BUYER BEWARE

Now here's a fun Frenchy factoid. The French government is pretty sticky when it comes to sales. Say you owned a tacky tourist shop and wanted to slash prices on a boatload of Eiffel Tower key chains. Outside of specific time periods you'd have to ask for special permission and be prepared to participate in the national pastime here, administrative paperwork. There are even inspectors who randomly check *les magasins* to ensure they are red tag free. So, to avoid all that hassle, the shops put everything on sale during two periods of the year. From mid-January until mid-February, every store in France has their windows obstructed by huge banners saying *SOLDES*!! And the bargains are excellent, sometimes as much as 70 per cent off. Then they do it all again in June. It ends up creating a situation much like a big game hunt. People quietly stake out the stores, their eyes slowly surveying the lay of the land while honing in on their targets. They take mental notes and on sale day, move in for the kill. Here in Semur it's a civilized affair, although I saw the situation in Paris on the news and I must say those Parisians really know the game.

I try to imagine this in North America, Boxing Day and Black Friday every day for a month, twice a year. Lives would be lost, states of emergency declared, the National Guard and UN Peacekeepers marching in the streets. The hospitals would be filled with women recovering from scratching each others eyes out over a pair of Jimmy Choo shoes reduced by 60 per cent. Even my own sister would slay me if I got in her way on this one. But it doesn't matter a row of beans to me now because unless it's 100 per cent off, I'm not buying. I will admit it's more than a little heartbreaking to know that everything in Paris, only a short train ride away, is being offered at rock bottom prices. In my former life I would have indulged in a little something, a pair of shoes, a scarf, maybe a new purse. All things I don't need. But still, there's always that at-that-price-it-would-be-irresponsible-not-to thinking, a trap I've fallen into many times before. And Neil, who has never paid full price for anything in his life, is often the one who drags me in. He once spent an hour convincing me that I was actually saving money by buying an outrageously expensive bag because it was on sale.

I guess I was dazzled by his masculine logic because it's currently in my closet. Now, unless it's food or deodorant on sale, spending never equals saving. Oh, listen to me — so sensible, so wise, so above the material wars. Now that's a laugh. If I had a paying job I'd be in full combat mode in the streets of Paris, head to toe camouflage, rifle in one hand, Visa in the other. I love the smell of Louis Vuitton in the morning.

SPEAKING IN TONGUES

Language update: I continue to suck. If I knew any French swear words, I'd say them, multiple times. Every time I think I'm making progress I get whacked in the forehead, hard and fast. Pharmacy woman is killing me. It was torture to see her even once after the whole *vaginale* debacle, but now every single time I go in she just happens to serve me. I ask for basic items in what in my estimation is perfect French and, as usual, she rapid-fires ten questions just above a whisper. Then she becomes impatient as I struggle for answers. I suspect she's actually from Manchester and is deliberately trying to drive me to the brink.

But the worst was a dinner party a few nights ago. This was a fairly upscale affair with eight people in total, all talking at once in a large space with a distinct echo. Everyone was *très chic* and my nervous state was enhanced by the fact that the mayor himself was serving the *foie gras* with red wine and onion *confiture* appetizer. I sat up straight, smiled a lot and made several valiant attempts to interact like I normally would. Nothing, crickets. Then finally I heard the mayor say a word I recognized. *Phoque.* He was talking about the seal hunt. Now here was something. This is a topic that my people know well and will not be debated here. We know the truth about it, others don't. End of story. Whether I was impassioned by my heritage or simply by a word that I actually recognized doesn't really matter at this point. All I can say is that I got riled up (likely tame by French standards) and finished the whole thing off by referring to Paul McCartney as a total ignoramus. Oh, the queen of restraint, me.

It was a beautiful party, but by the end I was all in and totally discouraged about the language. All I could think was I will never learn this mess well enough to secure a second invite anywhere. Intellectually I know all the right things to say to myself. These things take time. Assimilating to a new culture is one of the most difficult things to do. But I can't stand being excluded from witty banter. I think the worst is when everyone bursts into raucous laughter and I'm sitting there wondering what's so funny. It's like showing up for the shindig only to have some snooty 18-year-old hostess say you're not on the list.

I suppose there's nothing to do but keep at it with CDs, books, lessons, practice and perhaps a little intervention from above. At this point I'd be happy to resume my previous role as the woman who says inappropriate shit on a regular basis. Is it too much to ask the gods to rub a bit of garlic on my foot and serve it to me on a silver platter?

Bon Courage

The dreaded 15th of January is nigh. Even before we left for France this date has been an ever-present whisper of doom floating around in my head. Tomorrow Neil begins his long journey back to Canada. Poor man, he's been run ragged all week preparing for his monster workweek across the pond, but someone has to pay the bills and I nominate him. But what about me? I'm the one being abandoned in the land of butter and verbs to fend for myself, woman vs. wild, without so much as a vague clue how to communicate beyond, "I'll have all remaining *croissants* in the bakery please." It's just not safe. Yesterday I left a folder in the unlocked car with all our banking information inside — account numbers, codes, everything. Just the other day I broke off a cork in a very nice bottle of wine and it was almost ruined. Last night I left the front door unlocked all night. Does this sound like a person who can be left unattended?

I was fine until my bilingual neighbour, who knows every single thing there is to know about Semur, had to leave town unexpectedly for two weeks. She was my go-to gal in case of disaster. But as always, there's an upside. I get the whole bed to myself without having to turn the snoring beast beside me every couple of hours like a giant rotisserie chicken. I get to pick the movies so I can guarantee myself a *Matrix*-free week. Also, for some strange reason, when Neil's not here there's far less laundry to do. Still, there is the river that's rising by the hour, the watery cave, and the threat of starvation to contend with. But more than that, it's about being by myself for a full week. I know all the parents out there are pulling their hair out and would kill for a week by themselves. For me it's really about missing my sidekick. I realized that in almost ten years we've never been apart for more than a couple of days at a time. I'll just miss him. But I'm supposed to be challenging myself in every way possible. I know I'm tougher than I think I am so bring it on I say. If anyone's looking for me, I'll be locked in the bathroom.

DRIVEN TO DISTRACTION

Who has time to feel frightened and forsaken with a calendar as full as mine? The best defense against loneliness, fear and panic is to keep yourself occupied. Or when all else fails get someone else to do it for you, an approach I favour for just about anything in life.

My first night of solitude was easy. I cleaned myself up and joined my new friend Francis, a dapper retired English teacher and master gardener, to take in a Parisian string trio at the tiny town theatre. It's such a blessing to hear world-class musicians this way. My French teacher Patricia was with us, and when I told her I was on my own she offered to take me on a field trip to Beaune for a bit of cultural exchange—a badly needed haircut. I imagine she thinks this will make up for her springing a whole new verb tense on me the other day. She's a fascinating woman who previously ran a bed and breakfast in the Loire Valley for many years and taught language courses for multinational corporations. She's ripping apart a big house here in Semur having just finished converting a riverside ruin into a sweet vacation cottage. She spent Christmas touring Morocco by camel and sleeping in a tent in the desert and she's lived everywhere from Virginia to Portugal. Now she is starting an immersion language program here in town, which will apparently include makeovers for women abandoned by their husbands.

Barring any unforeseen disaster the rest of my week should be smooth sailing. I have a coffee date with our new friend Anne, who was born and raised near Chicago. In the early '60s she met her Swiss husband Michel, a gifted painter, and they settled in Burgundy to live off the land, hippie-style. And I have a lunch date with Jacqueline, who I'm excited about getting to know better. I'm dying to hear all about her life in Paris where she was once a model (finally a woman as tall as I am). She also sold luxury Parisian apartments before setting up her lingerie shop here in Semur, and I imagine she has a story or two to tell.

Of course, there's a mountain of French study to get through, boxes and boxes of cereal to eat and toilets to clean. It's a non-stop barrage of *bonne vivante* activities. Before I know it Sunday will be here when I know there's something else I have to do; I just can't recall it at the moment. Let me check my calendar. Oh yes, there it is, "pick Neil up at train station." If anyone's buying what I'm selling with that one, then I'm a better BS artist than I thought.

Co-Dependency

The King has returned and once more peace reigns in the palace. So happy was the Queen to receive him. I survived, of course I did, but I will say that his absence got me to thinking about this sense of dependency to which I have previously referred. I now know that I can be in France on my own, I just don't like it. Apart from all the love business, it's just easier when Rusty's around as he allows for the convenient division of labour or, in my case, the absolute delegation of duties.

The other day I was talking to an American man here and when I told him about my fear of being here on my own, he simply didn't believe me. He told me it was not possible as I came across as such an "independent woman." This is a phrase I've heard all my life and it's always confused me. It is almost always used to characterize women. You never hear, "Oh, he's very independent," (Mommy groups do not count). And independent as opposed to what … tethered?

Then a friend of mine gave me the gears when I told her of my misgivings about being here without Neil. She expressed her disappointment in me for becoming so dependent on a man and for single handedly bringing down the feminist movement. Before she called Ms. Steinem to turn me in, I tried to explain. I told her that I choose to see my relationship with Neil as mutually parasitic. Yes, I need him for many a thing, but in other ways he needs me too. For example, stain removal. If one desires the knowledge of what Neil has eaten in a day one need only sweep one's gaze over his shirt. Breakfast will be found near the belt, while dinner is always slightly higher. Some people carry those Epi-Pens for their life threatening allergies. He needs a Tide stick.

Then there was the time I found this grown man, a man who can do calculus in his head, standing naked at the top of the stairs with the shower running, his voice cracking with alarm, "Bobbi, I'm out of soap!" Of course, I directed him to the magic cupboard found in every house that seems to fall within the domain of those with ovaries—the linen closet. Finally, I am the chief of "have you seen my…?" Apparently I'm the only one who's aware of the location of everything we own. So all this will need to be kept in mind as come April we do it all over again. Me, starving, mute, paralyzed with fear of water both inside and outside the little French house, and him, parading about Canada sporting the latest foodwear with no soap in sight.

THE PLOT THICKENS

Whenever god has laughed at my plans in the past it's always been a kind and gentle chuckle, just to remind me of my place in things. But today the cackling from the great beyond is positively deafening. I find it convenient to direct blame towards a deity when I've just made one of the most startling decisions of my life.

Behind the scenes and little by little, Neil and I have been moving forward with our work here in France. Day by day we were discovering what our new life would be like. And while it began peacefully and full of promise, as the bigger picture came into view, I began to have some serious doubts. The more I saw, the more uncomfortable I felt. I could see that come high season, my life would be relentlessly hectic, 24 hours a day, seven days a week. I kept my apprehension to myself, wrote it off as new career jitters and hoped it would go away. It did not, and by the time Neil left for Canada, I was incredibly conflicted. I decided that some time on my own was the perfect opportunity to sort it all out.

I gave myself a thorough assessment. I took myself back to the days when I was gainfully employed and I remembered what it was about all those kids that impressed me so much. It was how carefully they considered their futures; their tireless evaluation of all the options before them. It was their clear knowledge, even in the context of significant illness, that the decisions they made would forever alter the courses of their lives. They knew that if they got it wrong at the beginning, it would be wrong at the end. They also knew that the only opinions that really mattered were their own. Thankfully, the concept of doing things simply because they are expected has been lost on this generation. I somehow missed this my first go around, but there was no way I was missing it now.

I methodically examined my resistance and, just for the record, excessive laziness was ruled out as the culprit. Yes, I came to France committed to making this opportunity work. And yes, I cut every cord possible to be free to focus on this new beginning. But instead of seeing all that as an imperative to continue, I saw it as all the more reason to make sure I didn't find myself right back where I started, locked into a life that didn't fit me.

In the end my choice was less about rational method and more about intuition. I just knew this path was not the right one; that it had to be a means to another end. So, once I had convinced myself, all that remained was to convince one other person. Despite my many years of breaking bad news to people I can honestly say the thought of handing this little gem to Neil made me slightly dizzy.

Once he settled in after his big week in Canada, we sat down for the talk. But before I could even get into my concerns he told me that he was having second thoughts about our venture. He had been offered an opportunity with a new client in Canada that he really wanted to pursue but he had no idea how to make it all work without making his life all about work. He had come to the same conclusion I had. In that moment I knew once and for all that my intuition was reliable. After all, it was what had led me to him.

Well, I always say you're never safe from surprise until you're dead. So where does all this leave me exactly? I'd say nowhere. I am now officially adrift, a broad abroad with no Plan B. As for what's next, I have no answer. The immediate plan is to keep calm and carry on wrestling with vocabulary. I suspect the ability to participate in a basic conversation is a requirement for most jobs around here and I'll need all the help I can get. It's not like I have a wide range of experience to fall back on, although I did work at a video store when I was in high school. Unless there's a shop on the Rue de la Liberté that rents English movies to suicidal teenagers, I'm shit out of luck. I suppose I could just continue to be a kept woman. Of course such a situation is so far beneath me and yet so far, it's not half bad.

Intuition aside, I tend to have a high need for the known and limited knowledge of possible outcomes represents uncharted waters for me. But now I find myself floating in a sea of the unpredictable. Obviously, without the promise of a career here in France, everything changes for me. It also makes house buying all the more difficult. We're still waiting to hear from the second bank on the Wreck which we now understand from the locals would take at least a year to 18 months to renovate. I'm not sure I can think about what will be happening in a year and a half. I don't even know what's happening next week. We've managed to negotiate to stay in this house until September, so that takes a little pressure off. But I'm surprised that

I don't feel more concerned than I do. It's the strangest thing. It's exactly the way I felt before I left Canada. I'm aware that things are happening but I'm oddly disconnected and willing to step back a little and see how it all plays out. Hopefully, an opportunity for me to make a living will make an appearance, as will the lodging fairy.

I'll have to put this dilemma out into the universe and see what comes back to me. I'll make lemons from lemonade. The world is my oyster. This will turn out to be the best thing that's ever happened to me. Everything unfolds as it's supposed to. Where's the wine? It's flowing like mud around here.

FEBRUARY

The Real Housewife
of Semur-en-Auxois

So here I am, supposedly living the dream. The trouble is I'm not quite sure yet what the dream actually is. The property management idea was pretty much the only one I had. Now I'm left with The Question. What's an unemployed unilingual psychiatrist in the middle of France to do with her time? Now that Neil has more work than he originally anticipated, he spends most of his day up in his makeshift office, which I try to avoid. Obviously I don't wish to disturb him in the sacred place where his big ideas generate small bits of coloured paper that can be exchanged for food, heat and Kindle books. And, like every office he's ever had, it's a space that somehow, without warning, becomes overtaken by disarray and makes me feel sweaty and vaguely faint. Despite this, most days I fear that I might have to duct tape myself to my chair to prevent me racing up the stairs every half hour to show him the frivolity I've just unearthed on Twitter. Clearly I need to flesh out my role in the new regime, so I sat down with *mon amour* to discuss just how this was going to play out.

We decided that I would keep on with the laundry, oh a big surprise that one. Also I will do the housecleaning, dare to dream I say, and be chief of supply management, the duties of which are noticing that we are low on toilet paper and adding it to the shopping list. It was a very interesting chat. He seems very pleased with this "new" arrangement. To me it feels quite uneven. He works a lot and I just keep doing things I've always done.

The potential drawback here is somehow sliding into a permanent arrangement that sees me becoming a servant for my husband. But what if I just saw it for what it is? Not a woman who is subservient to her husband, nor a man who expects his wife to serve. Rather two people trying to figure out how to wear this new life; two partners who have come to an agreement. We remain equal in all things, respectful of one another's tasks and each other's role in things. Why, just last night you could've cut the equality with a knife when my better two-thirds turned to me and said, "How about giving me a pedicure?"

WRECKLESS

While my career plans have changed radically, other areas of my life haven't changed in the slightest. We are still waiting to hear from the second bank. Today I spent an hour filling out medical questionnaires for mortgage insurance. Now I already have insurance up the wazoo in Canada, but French law says no French insurance, no Wreck, probably not a bad policy given my state of affairs. After all this finagling I'm not even sure I want it anymore. Just to recap, we've been at this since early October. With the benefit of time and distance, it's starting to feel foolhardy. There's nothing quite like signing documents you can't understand to stir up a bit of caution. It's absurd really, signing and initialling very official looking papers based on having only the gist of things. Of course I've done it many times before in Canada. I mean does anyone actually read every word of all the papers involved in a real estate deal? Not that I'm advising this, I'm just talking about how I tend to do things. Real estate, divorce, who has time for all the jargon?

Now that any real income for me seems far off, maybe abandoning the Wreck is the smart thing to do. While we wait for yet another bank to determine if we are indeed too rickety for their tastes we'll poke around for other options. On Saturday we're going to see a place that's supposedly all done. Nothing to do but unpack, hang a few pictures and *voilà*, instant life in France. See, I could get into that. After all the house drama we've created over the years, I wonder if two compulsive changers can renovate themselves into people who can just leave well enough alone?

Certainly this morning it was clear that we're not entirely prepared to change our barrel ahead approach as we signed papers that agree to who knows what. For all I know we've offered ourselves to be sacrificed at the next medieval feast here in the village. I'm not worried. There's no way they've got a spit long enough for me. As for Neil, he's a good bet, tender and sweet.

Warning:
Giraffe Crossing

When I was a kid my parents took me to Disney World and I remember those signs that said You Must Be This Tall To Enjoy This Ride, signs that never once excluded my gangly self. Perhaps there should be a big sign at the French border that says You Must Be This Short To Shower Here.

We visited the elusive no work required property, which was charming enough despite the dirt and dust from being closed up for so long. It had an exposed wall of stone, an open fireplace, great views and even a large office space for the one of us who actually works. So far, so good I thought, lots of cleaning and only one bright orange wall to paint. For us, small *pommes de terre*. But on the second floor things went awry. Instead of two decent sized bedrooms there were three small, weirdly shaped rooms with very low beams. Okay, I can live with that, I thought, I'll just take my helmet off when we invite people for dinner. Then the bathrooms, plural. Well, now we're talking. I always say the success of every relationship depends on an extra toilet. Of course good personal hygiene also helps maintain domestic bliss and therein lies the problem. The slope of the ceiling in the showers is not giraffe friendly. Particularly so if you are one that has plates and screws in your neck that prevent even the simple task of draining the last drop from a skinny wine glass. So walk away or rip them out and start over. Is there no end to this silliness for us? But in a town with so few possibilities, all must be considered carefully.

So we're actually thinking about this one long and hard. Unless I shrink four inches over the next couple of weeks, I might find myself renovating, albeit on a much smaller scale. Smaller scale. Somehow this phrase is not the least bit reassuring. From where I stand it doesn't make a damn bit of difference if I'm in quicksand up to my ankles or up to my neck, no matter how great the distance between them.

BREATHE IN,
BREATHE OUT

Meanwhile it's been grey and gloomy here since winter began. I've never seen such persistent weather in my life. The temperature goes up and down but the skies remain dark, making the town seem a little shabby and sad. I think we've seen the sun twice since late October. But this morning I woke to Neil raving about a yellow glowing object in an oddly blue sky and I thought a road trip was in order. We hopped in our little *voiture* and visited a few nearby villages and our spirits brightened considerably.

And while I'm in the car, allow me to veer off for just a minute. For some reason, I can't seem to stay awake for more than ten minutes as a passenger over here. This is a completely new experience for me so we think it has something to do with the engine vibrations or maybe the diesel fumes, hence Neil's latest term of endearment for me, diesel head. Picture me barely conscious but desperately trying to stay awake so I don't miss a single bit of France. I resist it with all my might, my head bobbing and drifting to the side until it finally hits the window, snapping me back from a dream like state with a snort, followed by me shouting, "What did I miss?" Then, 30 seconds later, it starts all over again and lasts for as long as it takes for us to get there. Neil thinks it's *très amusant* but for me it's *très frustrant*. By the time we get to wherever we're going I'm like a wet noodle.

So we were driving home after our leisurely day and I was in fine form when Neil slammed on the brakes, yelling, "Did you see that?" I saw nothing but my life before my eyes but apparently we'd just missed hitting a large deer. At least now I was half awake to see what happened next. We picked up some speed, rounded a corner and there, in the middle of the road, stood three men with their arms in the air. In my stuporous state I wondered what the odds were of them all being dressed alike. We stopped and the officer walked up to the window and asked Neil a question. I have no idea what. Between my fuzzy head and the French I didn't have a hope of knowing what the hell was going on. Although Neil's emphatic, "*Non, Monsieur,*" did register with me. And I perked up considerably when I saw him come face to face with a breathalyzer.

Of course being the ever-helpful wife I added, "Well, there was that glass of wine at lunch."

The officer guffawed at the couple of lightweights before him but persisted in waving the nozzle in Neil's face and instructed him to blow. It registered 0.0 and we were on our way. Afterwards it seemed so odd. No, "Let's see your licence and registration sir," no polite or impolite chitchat, just blow. Middle of a country road, five o'clock on a Saturday afternoon and the *gendarmes* were out doing roadblocks for boozers. Just before descending into oblivion and resuming my slack-jawed, drooling pose, I managed to slur, "I wonder why they singled us out?"

ZEN AND THE ART OF MACARON MAINTENANCE

The Great Canadian Purge was merciless. Not even my precious book collection survived. Out they went, Pablo Neruda, Carol Shields, Henry James. Even David Sedaris didn't make the cut. I kept one book and one book only, *The Places That Scare You: A Guide To Fearlessness in Difficult Times* by Pema Chödrön, a Buddhist nun who teaches at a Tibetan monastery in, of all places, Cape Breton, Nova Scotia. The reasons I kept this one for my current caper should be fairly obvious.

Well, today's a day when I wish I still had my faithful admin assistant Bonny with me. I'd race up to her yelling, "Get me Pema Chödrön on the phone right now! While you're at it, see where Karen Maezen Miller is and what the Dalai Lama's up to, because I have single-handedly discovered the pathway to inner peace." But first let me explain my terms of enlightenment. The answer came to me after a long period of, let's call it reflection, that involved lounging in bed for half the day, then sitting in a chair for the other half followed by some quality time on the couch, ending with a return to bed. Cripes, this inner peace is hard work.

I started with thinking about how I ended up here; about how I happened to find myself in a small town in France; about how I wound up jobless, bookless, hairless. Then I launched into pondering the future. What will become of me? What if I can't ever speak French any better than I do today? What if I get really sick over here? What if I have nowhere to live come September? What if skinny jeans stay in style forever? As usual, I let my brain run on autopilot and propel me into a state of absolute paralysis. It was in this moment of self-generated turmoil that the meaning of life revealed itself to me. My husband passed me these …

Macarons. The famous French cookie with its egg shell-like crust and delicate meringue texture followed by a layer of dark chocolate *crème* that would arrest even the most rampant stream of consciousness. These are no ordinary *macarons*. These are the Semur version and no words can capture their power. Butter and cocoa, the only two things required to ease the tortured soul.

I realized that every single decision I've ever made has led me to this moment, to these cookies. Today, the past and future are not my business. There is only the now of *macarons*. I asked the *macaron*, "What the hell am I doing here?" And the *macaron* said, "You think too much. Shut up and eat."

Town and Country

Almost every weekend now there's a distant plume of smoke that releases the sharp aroma of chestnut wood that will forever be locked in my senses as France. So when the lovely Anne and Michel offered us a most intriguing invitation, "Please come to our fire on Sunday," I thought call me Smoky the Giraffe, I'm in.

We presented ourselves in our puffy down coats, fleece gloves and fur lined winter boots and were welcomed by a local man who looked us up and down and declared, "You two look very urban." We're Canadians, what do you expect? We spend half the year in below zero weather so to me a metallic silver North Face coat is entirely acceptable gear for any occasion. But who the hell knows what to wear to a bonfire in the French countryside? Apparently everyone at le cookout. I could immediately see that we were lacking the tweed, wool and rubber that would have allowed us to blend in. Quite excitedly, Neil turned to me, "I'm going to have to get a whole country ensemble." Ah, this explains the many times our gay friends have reacted to my husband with a raised eyebrow and a hopeful smile. While I never doubt his loyalty to our side, he does show signs of wanting to defect from time to time — the key to the super husband I always say.

Of course this was no ordinary bonfire. It was a full-scale gourmet event. Fine wines in stemmed glasses, marinated chicken and local sausages tossed on the grill at the base of the fire, elaborate salads, baskets of *baguettes*, creamy cheeses on wooden boards, vanilla spice loaf, almond cake, *beignets* and, of course, espresso served fireside. *Mon Dieu*. I was expecting a wiener on a stick and a few marshmallows. What a day. I met a nine-year-old girl who speaks French and English and is now about to embark on a six-month exchange trip to Germany for the linguistic hat trick. I also met her mother, miraculously taller than me, who told me that she either has to buy her clothes in Germany or Switzerland or have them made by a *couturière*. Now I want a *couturière*, and the minute I can say it I'm getting one. Anne showed me her incredible *atelier* where she makes her stunning silver jewelry. And now I want an *atelier*. I can't actually make anything, I just want to say, "If you need me, I'll be in my *atelier* consulting with my *couturière*."

Despite the dreary weather, we were once again wrapped in the warmth of Burgundians. Maybe I'll scrap this whole town concept and become a country girl. At least I know who'll help me put together the perfect outfit.

MARCH

SHOCK TO THE SYSTEM

Now I knew before I moved to France that at some point I'd have to deal with the whole spine of glass issue. But for the last six months I've deluded myself that maybe it was all behind me, that by some miracle, retirement coupled with copious amounts of pastry and wine had cured me of my woes. That is, until I woke up one day and could no longer move my head. Privacy desires aside, I can endure some indecent exposure for the sake of international relations and cultural exchange. I'll skip the gory details and stick to the diving-into-the-medical-system-in-a-foreign-country ones. And oh what a system it is.

My week was a full out onslaught of tests and examinations that started with a trip to the local family doctor, who referred me to a neurologist in Dijon. Just three days later I was sitting on a velvet baroque chair in his office. I can almost hear Canadians gasping in amazement. When things got a little worse, I wound up in the local ER. After five minutes of waiting, a very pleasant young doctor examined me and ordered an X-ray and a CT scan. Forty-five minutes later I was walking to the car with the films in my hand. I hope none of the Canadians hit their heads as they pass out cold-junk on the floor from this one.

As is par for the course for me, an MRI was ordered, for which I waited a total of six days. In addition to a large hospital, Semur has its own ritzy radiology clinic, set in the middle of a field and completely funded by the state, where you can walk in and make an appointment for an ultrasound or a mammogram for whenever it's convenient for you. But the nearest MRI is located in Chenove, about a 40-minute drive from Semur. The clinic is exclusively for MRI examinations and, *bien sûr*, is named after a wine. Ten minutes after my scan, I met with the radiologist who gave me a full verbal report (in French, naturally), but I was too impressed by the process to be concerned. I was then handed a written report along with CDs of the scan tucked into a glossy folder, all for a little more than half the cost in Canada. All medical reporting here is done this way. Anytime something gets poked, prodded, swabbed or scraped, the results are either provided immediately or mailed to your home the minute they are available. I suspect by now any Canadian reading this has succumbed to an irreversible state of shock.

As a physician, I was astounded by the efficiency of this public system. I was equally impressed by the pleasant and cordial manner of the health care personnel here. The morale seems high and it appears to be quite important to them that they offer patients high quality service. I too must remember to be courteous when I craft my letter to the Canadian minister of health and refrain from closing with, "I suggest you bureaucratic meatheads stop discussing it to death, get on a goddamn plane and let the French show you how it's done."

Thankfully, it looks like I'm going to recover without having to meet any French surgeons. While I was certainly unhappy to need it, I was more than happy to have a first-hand experience of this famous system. On the whole, I'd say the best part of the whole rigmarole was going *sans* one of those wretched hospital gowns, as I tend not to do well with arse-to-the-world situations. Here in France, they wouldn't dream of requiring their patients to wear such distasteful garb. Instead, all that's needed is the removal of clothing that has any metal. They know how to do it all right, I thought as the handsome French technician in his designer jeans and patent leather shoes escorted me to the scanning room. How sophisticated, how extraordinarily dignified, to saunter down a cold corridor under fluorescent lighting wearing a grey cashmere sweater, black tube socks and $1.99 blue cotton underpants.

La Man Cave

I'm not up to 100 per cent but at least I'm up and about. After four weeks of taking it easy, also known as lying on a bed and staring at the ceiling until you descend into madness, I'm finally getting out of the house. And not a moment too soon, because the weather is suddenly glorious. Who knew that there are places in the world where spring actually arrives before the end of May? Why, it seems like only yesterday that I rolled out of my tent in Terra Nova Park on May 24th weekend, hungover and blue from the cold, into half a foot of snow. Ah, those were the days. Here in Semur, the forsythia is in bloom, the willow trees are coming to life and the window boxes are already full of flowers. So spine be damned, a walk was in order.

We stopped in front of the Wreck for a moment and in the warm sunshine we dreamed of the finished product for the millionth time. Everything seems easy in the first blush of spring. A little further up the street we stopped to admire a fully renovated house when, out of nowhere, a man appeared who greeted us enthusiastically, congratulated us on moving to France and asked us what we liked about his house. Oh, where to start? He told us that the house dates back to the 1600s and then he bolted down the hill to get his keys because we just had to see his cave. He raced back like an excited child, swung open the doors and *voilà, la cave*, which, as far as I could tell, was basically a garage with a curved stone ceiling. Inside there were tools and all kinds of crap that one usually finds in places where cars are supposed to be kept. I was a bit underwhelmed to say the least. I was thinking, this is your man cave? Where's your massive flat screen television and framed Montreal Canadiens jersey? Then I looked a little closer and behind all the rakes and shovels, resting against the dark walls, were bottles and bottles of wine, too many to count. He went to the back wall where there was a large piece of cloth hanging in front of several milk crates. He reached in behind and with dramatic flair started pulling out wine from his collection, dusty bottles from the '40s to the '80s with beautifully ornate labels from all over France.

Now North American men, take note. This is a man cave. Not some panelled rec room with orange shag carpet, a bar with brown vinyl padding, a neon beer sign and posters of NASCAR drivers. Not that I would frown on such a room. I'm not that one of those wives who tries to own every inch of the house. I've decided that my man can have a room all for himself if he wants, his very own sanctuary, a mantuary if you will, and he can fill it with any vintage he likes.

THE OLD GREY MARE

According to Wikipedia, 43 years ago today GM produced its 100 millionth car and, according to my mother, on the very same day, she produced me.

I'm 43 but I don't look a day over 55. For as long as I can remember, I've always taken the day off work, the one day a year when I can do whatever the hell I please. So I called Neil to tell him that I wouldn't be coming in to do the laundry or clean the bathroom. I also told him that I needed his Visa number and I got busy with the very important business of trolling the web for the perfect present.

I've decided that I want a pair of pretty French shoes for summer. Girly shoes, not my usual orthopedic canoes, but strappy lady shoes that require nail polish and maybe even a flowy skirt. Bear in mind that the last time I wore a dress there was a guy in a dark suit next to me vowing to make my dinner for the rest of his life. I bookmarked a few pairs and set off for a walk. After scaling the stone stairs and navigating century-old cobblestone streets, all while avoiding pile after pile of dog poop, it occurred to me that maybe shiny red sandals are more than a little ambitious for my *petite ville* life. And as I walked to the edge of town and saw what my neighbours were wearing I realized that I might need to rethink my plans for my husband's money.

Maybe I'm not just another year older. Maybe I'm actually getting wiser in my middle age. After chatting a bit with these gals, it dawned on me that I don't need new shoes to fit in. I can blend in without spending a dime.

I have to admit the resemblance is uncanny. Next time I see her, I have to remember to ask her who cuts her hair.

THE RUBBER STAMP

I've finally learned how long it takes for two Canadians to get approved for a mortgage in France. To be fair, I have no idea how long it takes for immigrants in Canada, something to think about, but here it takes six months. Six bloody months. While I was laying in the MRI scanner last week, the bank manager called Neil with the good news. It's a good thing I was confined within a giant magnetic tube. All I could think of was that scene in *Terms Of Endearment* where Shirley MacLaine runs around the hospital screaming like a bedraggled banshee, "GIVE MY DAUGHTER THE SHOT!" Well, that would have been me grabbing anyone I saw by the lapels screaming, "GIVE ME THE FRENCH WORD FOR IRONY!" Turns out it's *ironie*. Of course it is.

Now I say irony because now that we have a mortgage we have nothing to buy. We had been holding back a little for a couple of reasons. The word on the street was that the seller of the Wreck wanted to up the already high price. *Mais oui*, spring is here and soon foreigners will turn to thinking about French Wreck-buying, so why not jack it up? Good for her, but not so good for us. And then there was the plumbing thing. Every time we asked someone about the extrusion path of excrement, the answer was the same: somewhere, who knows? I know where this is going. Half the budget will get eaten up with carving sewer lines through the granite hill that the house sits on, so we'll know where our food goes but have no kitchen to make any.

While all the waiting was going on we had gone to see an apartment for rent, which didn't work for us but presented renting as a viable option. After plenty of discussion we came to the conclusion that renting was indeed the path to continued mental health. No pressure, no long-term commitment and plenty of time to kick back and see what happens. We know now (I knew all along) that this is the truly sensible thing to do, and I was so proud of us saying no to madness and yes to sanity. But as usual, it was only temporary sanity. Once the mortgage approval came through, with a limited time to either accept or not, we went right back to the house idea. What a pair of morons, but after six months of tireless effort it felt wrong not to put it to use somehow.

Here's where it gets really interesting. While we figure out this house issue we need to hedge our bets. At the very least we'll need somewhere to live if the renovation ever actually comes to pass. Now there is a whole new approval process that requires the same mountain of paperwork to determine if we're fit to be renters here in France. And here I thought I was done seeking the approval of others. As for the application for a simple life ... denied.

Giraffe of Steel

Everyone had a favourite superhero. I used to dream of being Wonder Woman. But now that I'm a woman myself, I wonder how I ever took a superhero in a bustier and satin underpants seriously. How can you be expected to stave off criminal masterminds with satin panties wedged half-way up your arse and a boob hanging out? Anyway, the point is that I too am a superhero. Today I managed to successfully mail a package at the post office all by myself. Oh I can just imagine the ribbing I'd receive from my friends at home. I mean who the hell can't mail a parcel? But I challenge anyone to head on up to the local UPS and try to mail a package in Swahili. Trust me, it's major.

Fuelled by my superhuman success, I sauntered down to the physio-therapy clinic to rustle up a *rendez-vous* with a gal reportedly skilled with glass spines. But by the time I got to the door my strength had faded and I started my internal retreat. It's just so much easier to charm Neil into doing everything for me. I copied down the phone number and walked away. But something wasn't quite right. I started thinking about how busy my sugar daddy is these days and that nag called my conscience started whispering in my ear. So, I summoned the forces necessary to go back and, shazam! I managed to have a whole conversation (sort of) and I walked out with an appointment for next week. Well slap my arse and call me Harry! I practically skipped down the street. The sun was shining, the breeze was warm, the cherry trees in the churchyard were in full bloom and I had just saved civilization.

But my most heroic act was the defeat of the villainous French dinner party. We were invited to dine with a woman from the mayor's office to be introduced to another foreigner, a South African architect with plans to transform Semur's ancient hospital into a luxury four-star hotel and spa. I understood about a third of everything that was said (a personal best for me) and I don't mind saying I was feeling rather full of myself. It was a miracle I didn't break into a soliloquy from Hamlet. I was solid as a rock until our hostess said something about six months followed by *incroyable*. Blank stare. What the hell was she saying? Finally, after a long pause, Neil leaned in, "She said it's incredible how much French you have learned in six months." He's well acquainted with marriage by now so he didn't add "you doofus" at the end. What can I say? Even Superman had kryptonite.

APRIL

By the Skin
of My Teeth

So here's something I've learned about living in a foreign language: context is everything. I had already learned that plenty of understanding comes less from words than gestures and facial expressions, but I didn't realize how much I'd been getting by with full-scale theatrical productions of what I'm trying to say. Of course all this goes away when you're on the phone. Neil, with his Spanish, French and a bit of Italian just to show off, has always told me that he has great difficulty speaking any foreign language on the phone, which I never understood. Either you *parlez-vous* or you don't. I put it down to his fundamental weirdness when it comes to phone finesse. Here's a perfect example: he answers the phone. I wildly gesticulate how unavailable I am at the moment, which involves mouthing, "I'm in the shower," while rapidly sweeping my hand back and forth across my throat, which, as every single person on the planet knows, means I'm not here. He says, "Sorry, hold on a minute, Bobbi's trying to tell me something." I then politely say hello, my shoe goes sailing toward his head, and he looks confused. Every single time.

Well, it looks like a feed of crow is on my menu tonight as I just got off the phone with a receptionist at a dentist's office here in town and it was a narrow escape to be sure. The good news is I've reached my target heart rate for the day and lost a couple of pounds in sweat. The bad news is I have a whole new language challenge. Recent claims about my French progress were clearly exaggerated. I'd rehearsed everything I needed to say but I forgot that someone would be responding to me. Every time she spoke it was a stream of gobbledygook. But it takes more than that to keep me down. Being made fun of by snotty mainlanders your whole life eventually pays off. I just kept right on talking through all her sighs and audible eye rolls with no concern at all for her disdain, much like any Newfoundlander would behave when faced with an Air Canada employee. At the end of the day I'm the big winner and she can kiss my lily-white *derrière*. I've developed an empathic understanding of my husband's phone difficulties, plus I have a dental appointment at the end of May ... or a date on Saturday night with a dental hygienist named Celeste. Either way, not too shabby.

You Snooze,
You Lose

So while my clever husband and I conducted our great Wreck conversations, all those tremendous back and forth sessions of should we or shouldn't we, while we studied the town sewage line diagrams, while we considered how much we could save on the renovation using a DIY (also known as DIN—do it Neil) approach, something very interesting happened. We finally got a mortgage and within days of receiving it someone else swooped in and bought the house. To be honest, I'm relieved. I love when decisions are made for me as it leaves so much more time for other pressing matters, like eating and navel-gazing. I think it was meant to be because at the very moment the Wreck was snapped up from under our noses, we were advised that France has officially declared us fit to be renters.

The universe has spoken and I'm listening carefully for a change. We'll rent a place here and officially hit the longest period in our relationship without a major renovation. But I will have to keep an open mind with this. Having no income requires a fair bit of sacrifice and I'll have to learn to lower my standards accordingly. I bet it'll be easier than I expect. I'm not asking for much, just a place that's cozy, comfortable and easy to maintain. Maybe something like this little place in town …

Or maybe not. I'd need horses and footmen and scullery maids and quite frankly, I'm not sure I have the energy to break in a new staff. I'd have to stand on the balcony all day in jodhpurs and polished riding boots, my white chiffon scarf trailing behind me in the breeze, sipping an ice-cold cocktail while waiting for Neil to serve dinner on the terrace. Then after dinner, I'd have to change into one of my many gowns and stand motionless on the balcony gazing at the moon. Never mind the mortgage payments, it's the wardrobe that would put me under. No, maybe all I need right now is a place that is peaceful, a spiritual sanctuary if you will, somewhere I can sit quietly and wait for a sign of what to do.

Clearly someone is on to me. Maybe it's true what they say, everything happens for a reason. That house was simply not meant to be. Today I've learned that maybe, just maybe, Wreckless is the new sensible.

Sunny with a Chance
of Happiness

La vie goes on and the weather here seems to have taken a turn for the consistently beautiful, with relentless sunshine and temperatures soaring into the low 20s. Oh I'm excited about experiencing my first spring in Semur. Probably because growing up in the North Atlantic I had only heard of this "spring." Usually we had three nice days every second July between months of snow and ice and our other season called rain, drizzle and fog. It's not much better in Nova Scotia this time of year. Last check in Halifax it was five degrees with wet flurries, suckers. Never in my life have I gazed upon a bright green lawn that is long overdue for a mowing in the early days of April. Apparently this spring business can last for weeks and weeks, like say … the length of a season. Who knew? Clearly we'll need some time to adjust. We've left the snow tires on the car because, as every East Coast Canadian knows, a raging blizzard in the middle of May is not unheard of and always happens the day after you paid a couple of hundred bucks to have your bald, all-season radials put on.

The *Semurois* have obviously seen this weather phenomenon before. They've been gardening for weeks now. All their pots are full of flowers and their hedges have been trimmed. My flower rule has always been nothing goes in until the end of May, a lesson learned from many a frostbitten geranium. But because I'm a woman who likes to live on the edge, this weekend I'm off to pick up a few *fleurs* for the patio.

Of course not all things spring are lovely and peaceful. Here on the river we're surrounded by dozens of ducks now into their fourth week of robo-mating, quack whores the lot of them. Holy *merde*, what a drama and what a racket! The poor females are being chased to the point of desperation. The other day, one poor lady duck was so besieged by suitors that she flew smack into the house. It's quite a sight to see a full-grown duck splat herself, then slide down the full length of a glass door. She's fine, but she did look quite embarrassed.

Who knows if this will last? It's not for me to say; my job is simply to enjoy every minute of it, yet another benefit of unemployment. When I was slaving away in hospitals, I wonder how many gloriously warm April days I missed. Let me see. Seven years in Newfoundland followed by nine years in Nova Scotia. That makes exactly six days.

Closing Doors and Opening Windows

Something happened recently that caused me to stop eating for a minute and think. My two favourite activities, stuffing my face and turning a thought over and over until my head aches with the strain. There I was, minding my own business, heading home after a day of poking about rural France, when my old life reached out and smacked me in the face. We were whizzing around a corner as it came into view but somehow my brain was on autopilot and managed to piece together the necessary details. Without even thinking I told Neil to stop the car, and suddenly I was running toward her. An-all-too-familiar scene, a pale and shaking human being lying on the ground, blood all over her legs and terror all over her face and a few worried strangers doing their best to help. Cue my former life with, "I'm a doctor," a phrase as familiar to me as my own name. I determined that she'd fallen off her bike and was not seriously hurt. I told her that she would be all right and then the ambulance arrived. I walked back to the car, we motored on and I thought nothing more of it.

Later that night, I remembered that Neil had asked me when I was halfway out of the car if I was sure I wanted to get into this. I don't think I answered him. As I saw it, there was no choice. But now I'm not so sure. Did I really have any business being there? My response was so automatic, so instinctual, that I hadn't even stopped to consider it. What if she'd been severely injured? Would I have known what to do or would I have forgotten the very basics already? The point is, a decision will need to be made about this doctoring business and it's not a small one. After being away for a year or two, it takes a lot of effort to get back in the game—studying, refreshing, sometimes even taking exams and being approved by colleagues. I'm too lazy to learn French pronouns so I can hardly imagine having to face that debacle. Even if I fell out of love with France and returned to Canada, would I go back to a life in medicine? I don't know.

There's no measure of how wonderful it is to help people when they need it the most but there is also no measure of the bull*merde* that the business of medicine has become. I miss my patients and co-workers, but in all honesty the system is a situation best coped with by sticking a fork in one's eye. In July it will be a year since I resigned and I'll have to decide one way or the other. As I always say, no one likes to jump unless they've got a soft place to land. For now I've decided to just keep on eating. That way, no matter where I leap, my expanding arse will cushion the fall.

SQUARE ONE

When you leave one life behind it is inevitable that you have to start building another. So far it's been easy. We live here in a little house that has everything we could ask for—furniture, dishes, towels, even a flat-screen television. But now it's time to start thinking about moving on. First there was The Great Canadian Purge and now comes The Great French Acquisition. When I think about having to set up a house yet again I just want to crawl into bed with a couple of pounds of chocolate and an IV infusion of a nice cold Meursault. See this is when I wish I were Beyoncé or Gywneth Paltrow or some other queen of fabulous. I would click-clack around in my six-inch diamond encrusted platforms, bitch-slapping servants and screaming top lung about the chinchilla bedspread clashing with my hair. Or better yet, I could just jet off to my villa in Italy, play a few hands of poker with George Clooney and the gang, and arrive home to a fully arranged palatial abode.

But instead I spent last weekend in my orthopedic loafers and a de-cade-old jean jacket checking out discount dishes and linens at Ikea. On the one hand it's great fun, a chance to start all over and face the challenge of purchasing exactly what I need and not one thing more. On the other hand, when I think of how many times I've moved and how much I've sold or given away over the years, I get hives coupled with an intense compul-sion to stuff an entire cake in my mouth. This one will do just fine …

I've been doing a little digging through the things we brought from home and as I go through it now I wonder what I could have possibly been thinking at the time. *Par exemple*, I carefully ironed and vacuum packed my long-searched-for bed skirt. Very smart. Except that queen beds here are a different size and the bed skirt won't fit a French bed frame, so that was a stroke of genius now, wasn't it? Packed in with it I found a single white towel. Now what kind of birdbrain brings one lousy towel all the way across the Atlantic? Me.

So here we go again. We need just about everything so maybe the answer is to throw myself a shower. Instead of a bridal or baby shower I'll have one of those I Lost My Mind, Ran Away to France, Sold All My Shit and Now I Need All New Shit showers. That will look just beautiful embossed on an invitation.

MAY

CREATURE COMFORTS

Zut alors there's a lot to get used to living out here in the wilds of France. Perhaps I've already said this but the language is killing me, slowly but effectively. I went to the shoe store the other day and left empty handed and red faced from my ridiculous attempts at a basic conversation. Same *merde*, different day. But today I'm on about the critters.

I had no idea when I signed up for this that I was moving to a medieval zoo. Hairy pigs, goats and alpacas around the corner. Ducks frantically screwing and now pooping wherever they please as if they owned the place. They had better get it together *tout de suite* because I have two words for them, orange sauce. Now I've got giant snails, river bugs and mosquitoes by the thousands, bats swooping around my head at night, exotic horror film spiders in the bathtub, and the odd rat scurrying across the terrace chased by a huge black cat that frightens the life out of me every time it darts over my feet. Last night a pterodactylish moth bigger than my head appeared out of nowhere. It's like living in a Harry Potter book. But now we've reached a whole new level of vermin invasion.

This morning, as I innocently stepped out onto my sunny terrace, I was greeted by a loud buzzing. I looked down and there at my feet was a large dead bird covered in a swarm of black flies feasting on the carcass. Holy son of satan. I mean I'm all for this all god's creatures crap but Dr. Doolittle I am not. Who wants that mess on their doorstep? Oh, I know who does, my husband. Yesterday he came through the door practically bursting with excitement, "GUESS what I saw out in front of the house?" Ever the optimist, I was thinking a guy selling Miracle Whip but no such luck. "A snake," he said with a smile as wide as the sea. I suppressed my alarm and calmly replied, "What do you mean, like, a little skinny garden snake?" But I could tell by the look in his eyes that he was swept away by the love for anything gross that boys so often seem to share. "No, a real snake, like, four feet long, and it was all mashed up in the middle." Lovely. Apparently the hills are alive with *les serpents*. Neil will think he's died and gone to heaven. Later, as we set out on our daily walk, he was quite distracted by a desire to show me this mangled reptile and was disappointed to find it had since disappeared. "Oh no, somebody must have cleaned it up," he said sadly. Now if that's not a great date then I don't know what is. If I had a dollar for every smooth talker who tried to show me a limp snake …

SECRETS AND LIES

While narcissistic self-disclosure seems to have overtaken my life these days there is one piece of information I've kept under wraps. The secret is that for the past nine days I've been all by my lonesome, abandoned yet again. Neil's been off in Canada doing whatever he does to keep me in the scaled back style to which I am trying to become accustomed. What surprised me was that it wasn't remotely as terrifying as the last time. Of course this time there were a lot of things in my favour. The river has been reduced to a mere trickle, the weather has been glorious and I think I'm now able to communicate that I've fallen and I can't get up. I also had a lot more to do.

Anne came for a visit and presented me with beautiful silver earrings she'd made as a thank you for Neil's help with her computer. It seems I got the better end of that deal. I had a divine lunch served to me at the home of some new globe-trotting gourmet friends, then drinks with my new Irish friend Carmel at the *Café Des Arts*. Later in the week, there was more lovely lunching with my neighbour Elizabeth, and a dinner in town with my new physiotherapist, the young, adorable and very skilled Elodie without whom I couldn't move my head. A dinner, I might add, during which she and I spoke only French. Very simple and very slow French, but still a triumph to be sure.

On the whole, I did very well, I think. Although, there was the Chicken Incident. Convinced that I was now fully competent to live on my own, I decided I'd be bold and make myself some breaded chicken. I mean if I can manage a violently psychotic individual then surely a chicken breast shouldn't present a major problem. I was in the clear right until the clean-up when somehow the raw chickeny-eggy breading mess went flying all over every surface in sight. Because I am a germaphobic lunatic when it comes to dealing with raw poultry, I had to bleach the whole kitchen. I completely forgot about my chicken and finally removed it from the oven, charred into a black piece of concrete. Special K for dinner, again.

But here's the real shocker. While the cat's away the mouse will work. For almost three hours I was employed here in the village. Jacqueline sold her lingerie shop and I offered my services to assist with the inventory. Cut to a sunny cobblestone street, racks of clothing blowing in the breeze, cafés filled with people drinking espresso, pots and pots of flowers covering the sidewalk and then me, tallying fine French underwear while Jacqueline meets her clients with grace and elegance. There really is magic in the life of a French boutique. See, I'm all right here in the wilds of Burgundy alone. No problem whatsoever. Why, I could do this for another nine days. Who needs a brilliant and charming husband to cook and get groceries and answer the phone in case there's a French person calling? Not me baby. I'm as tough as snails.

HOUSEBOUND

As much as I fantasize about being one, I'm not the kind of girl who hops on a high-speed train to Paris with a moment's notice, and yet this week that's just what I did. While I'd love to say that I had a fitting at Chanel, the purpose of my travels was almost as good.

About a week ago, we had seen a truly magnificent apartment here in town. Quite simply it was the French apartment of my dreams. It's located in an ancient convent and after passing through the enormous exterior gates, past an enclosed gravel courtyard, I found myself in the building's foyer. It was like walking into a treasure cave. The floor was covered with ancient mosaics that led to a curved marble staircase, a work of art with its gold handrails and elaborately scrolled ironwork. I could have just camped out at the foot of the stairs and been happy. But once the agent led us through the apartment's towering ornate doors, I actually had to remind myself to keep breathing. Perfectly preserved herringbone oak floors, 13-foot ceilings, intricately carved mouldings that snaked their way from wall to ceiling, an antique marble fireplace, and a three sets of floor to ceiling French doors offering a view of the river below. It was as if it had been secretly plucked from an elegant Parisian address and then gently placed in the centre of this unassuming town. All my life I had longed to see one of these apartments up close, and now it was a signature away from being my new home.

The practicalities, however, were another matter altogether. The kitchen was literally the size of a closet, the bedroom was located right next to the main door of the building, there was no private outdoor space and the heating system was entirely inadequate for an apartment that had a living room, or should I say *salon*, with the dimensions of a ballroom. Not to mention the dilemma of furnishing a palace on an Ikea budget. But, like politicians in a brothel, we were so seduced by beauty that any drawbacks seemed negligible. We were about to sign the lease when during a lesson my French teacher just happened to say, "I know a guy who has a little house here coming up for rent. Let me call him." A visit was arranged within minutes and I prepared myself for the inevitable letdown I feel after seeing French houses. They're always drop dead gorgeous on the outside, all stone and shutters and gravel courtyards but one step inside and *la catastrophe*. Twice during our search we've encountered the much desired indoor doggie doo area.

But this house was a miracle. Sure, tiny but well designed and newly renovated (Neil, step away from the hammer) with two toilets (divorce team, stand down) and the tallest shower I've seen in France. The clincher was a completely private little *jardin* (currently a patch of weeds) with a stunning view of Semur's ancient church, all for less than we'd pay for a one-toilet studio in downtown Halifax. It was a long way from the grandeur of the elegant apartment, but in our hearts we knew we belonged there.

The house is an investment property owned by three Parisians so, loaded down with stacks of paper, we hopped on the first train to Paris to audition for the role of renters. We met two of them at a café and nervously began the story of how wonderful and reliable we are. One owner clearly thought we were a safe bet but the second, just off the night train from meetings in Rome, was harder to read. Their impressions of us were to be offered later to the third owner, who was in Vienna on business. Of course she was. What do these people do for a living? Anyway, now there are three more people in France who know every detail of our lives, down to the last euro.

I'm not used to all this being judged worthy business. What a sorry sight, two middle-aged people who have bought and sold ten houses between them checking their email every five minutes to see if they've been granted the title of tenants. Several harrowing days passed until we got the call to say we'd made the cut, and much rejoicing followed. I knew this whole moving to France idea was pure genius, which means it must have been my idea. I was ecstatic, swirling about in joyful rapture, until a dark wave of reality swept over me: I'm moving again. Psychiatrist, heal thyself.

LOVE AND THE CITY

Last week, after the meeting with our landlords, we took a long stroll though the streets of my favourite city. And as I gazed upon its beauty I thought it's likely a good thing I came to know Paris a bit later in life, now that I'm bitter and twisted—I mean, older and wiser. Who knows what effect it would have had on me when I was young and impressionable and single? It really is true when they say that Paris is ridiculously romantic. Of course they also say that the Frenchmen have the market cornered when it comes to sweeping the *mademoiselles* off their stilettos, and I've got it all figured out. It has nothing to do with ze Frenchmen at all. They just have a lot to work with. Take any guy in Paris, say this one, way off to the left ...

I have no idea who he is, some random guy who could be the world's biggest jackass and yet I guarantee that he could have any woman he wants in a state of rapture within three hours in this city, and here's why. He'll start off right where he is and pick up a few things for his mission …

After he's secured the posies, he'll go on to the next stall …

Here, he'll pick up a strand of chunky pearls that he'll just happen to have in his pocket when she answers the door because he knows she'll be wearing a little black dress. He also knows that as he's artfully closing the clasp around her neck, she is two martinis away from believing that she's Audrey Hepburn. And we all know where that's going.

Then he'll move on to the next stall …

He'll select the freshest and finest for his pre-dinner spread because he knows that the secret to snagging and snogging is all about his ability to cook. And then he'll suggest a midnight supper at this little place he knows …

I mean who could resist all this? Any schmuck could come off as suave with all this available to him. But one thing I know for sure: a man in a rundown bar in Nova Scotia, wearing a T-shirt full of holes while charming a jaded woman right out of contented singledom, he's got to be the real deal, and he knows it.

DeGaulle to Dog Doo

Maybe it's a desperate search for stability with all this moving lunacy or maybe it's the fact that I just have too much time on my hands, but for whatever reason I've decided I need a better understanding of this foreign land. Lately I'm getting more than I bargained for from a book written by two Canadian journalists, Jean-Benoît Nadeau & Julie Barlow, called *Sixty Million Frenchmen Can't Be Wrong*. It's an intelligent study of what makes the French so French, as if they should be anything else. Paid to travel all over France and write a big book report, where's that job now that I'm looking? While the book's cover suggests a light discussion of berets and *baguettes* nothing could be further from the truth. It's an enlightening and riveting (for geeks like me) treatise on every aspect of French history and culture. By the way, the authors do acknowledge the title borrowed from a Cole Porter song as fundamentally sexist. But blaming Porter and his era is a bit like me blaming France for my state of doughiness when it's quite obviously Neil's fault, but I digress.

I'm quickly becoming an expert in French culture:

History: complicated

Etiquette: fairly complicated

Judicial system: quite complicated

Education: significantly complicated

WWII and Algerian War: ridiculously complicated

Government: complicated beyond measure

Commitment of the French to loving, hating, defending and condemning France: simple

It's been incredibly useful for me to learn so much about this country. I now know more about France than I've ever known about Canada, which is embarrassing for sure. But then really what's to know? Beavers, maple syrup, saying you're sorry, recycling, hockey, hockey and more hockey, done. Canada's not hard to understand. It's a culture about ten minutes old, based on respect for any culture that happens to present itself, hence the marvelous Vietnamese, Thai and Indian restaurants from coast to coast. But one thing I've learned from living here, now solidified by this book, is that foreigners (me included) often forget that France has a culture as unique and strong as that found in Japan or Ethiopia or Nepal. The French have always been here and, as the book suggests, they are their own aboriginals. There's been no break in their long history and it seems there's only one way to truly become part of French society: adapt.

I suspect this is the beginning of a long education but I figure I'd better know what I'm getting into if I want to truly assimilate, one of the core principles of French culture. Of course it might have been smarter to read this book a little earlier, perhaps before deciding to discard my entire life and move here. For all I knew, it was custom for all unemployed psychiatrists to be publicly stripped naked and pelted with rotten fruit the first Tuesday of every month. Lucky for me, so far all that's really required is proficiency in the language. On second thought, I'm free on Tuesdays.

YOU CAN'T TAKE IT WITH YOU

Actually, in France you can. When we first saw the little house soon to be our new home, it was filled with another life. An enormous red sofa, toys, dishes and knickknacks, all the things that have now been stuffed into dozens of boxes and carted away. Today we're going back with only a measuring tape to see how our life will fit. While this is business as usual for most, for us it's a complete novelty. Normally we're dragging a group of contractors with us, deciding which walls are coming down, where to put the new kitchen, how to turn a closet into a bathroom, with plans to completely transform a house that was compelling enough to buy but not good enough to stay as it is. I'm absolutely overjoyed with this doing things like a normal person concept. Since seeing the house for the first time I've been basking in the glow of it, dancing about the countryside and congratulating myself on my undeniable brilliance.

But yesterday, I had a thought that stopped me cold as it dropped into my brain with a resounding thud. The kitchen. Now I know this seems incongruous to say the least. Why the hell am I concerned about a room so foreign to me that I knock before entering? Well, at our first visit the current tenant was kind enough to give us the full tour. And when I say kind, I mean nine months pregnant, choking with a cold, scrambling after her sugar-fuelled toddler, trying to pack as two Canadian strangers asked her every detail of her house.

Here in France, rental properties don't usually come fully loaded. Of course now that I have become a sophisticated European I knew that she'd be taking all the appliances with her. But I forgot to ask her if they were taking the kitchen as well. I can hear a collective "say what?" *Non, c'est vrai.* The French often take all their cabinets with them when they move. How they make that work remains a mystery to me, but the point is I was trying to take up as little of this woman's precious time as possible, so I left without this vital information. Now all I can think is please, please, please let me see cupboards when we open the door this afternoon. Apart from the obvious issues of time and money, designing, purchasing and installing a whole kitchen will totally offend my new "no renovation allowed" sensibilities. No, I'm serious, it will really disrupt my serenity and GODDAMN IT, NOBODY SCREWS WITH MY SERENITY!

CLOSE QUARTERS

I wonder what percentage of my life has now been spent on the business of dwellings. Of course, I blame it all on Neil and his love affair with tools and dust. It seems like the last ten years have been nothing but measurements, drywall, paint colours and appliance dimensions. Overall it's been loads of fun and profoundly educational, but make no mistake, it's a huge amount of work to renovate houses year in and year out, and that's not what I want my life to be now. I couldn't be happier about moving into a place where any form of destruction is actually prohibited by law.

As for our petite *maison*, or the housette, as I like to call it, I think when I first saw it I was so enchanted with the second toilet and the view from the terrace that I forgot to notice that it's the smallest house in France. The good news is that the kitchen cupboards are staying. The bad news is that there are only four of them. There's a sink and countertops but for everything else we're on our own. Neil, perhaps the only man alive who gets excited by ovens, has spent days researching French appliances. Yesterday you could have cut the romance with a hacksaw as we lay in bed talking about washer drum sizes before our eyes were even open. Next we'll move on to The Great French Furniture Hunt. We have some cash tucked away from the sale of our Canadian goods so we're fine on that front. The problem comes in trying to find things like a bed that fits a giraffe yet also fits under a medieval roof slope.

I suspect the majority of my time will now be divided between the hour-long drive to Ikea and the three hours it takes to find a parking space. It would be nice to romanticize all this and invent tales of picturesque drives to antique shops all over France but the reality is that we have about three weeks to get this together. Neil needs to have as little interruption as possible to his work and I need to have as little interruption as possible to his ability to make my dinner. Really what I want is to walk into one store, buy the contents of a house, have it all delivered that afternoon and sit back with a cold, congratulatory chardonnay. I'm trying to stay positive despite feeling slightly overwhelmed with it all. Utility and Internet setup in a foreign country, signing a lease in a foreign language, figuring out how to furnish tiny, awkwardly shaped rooms. Probably all of this is the least of my worries. What I should be working on is a plan for living in such a tight space with Big Red without causing bodily harm. At least when things get rough I'll have my own toilet to fall back on.

Middle Aged

With all the house mania going on around here lately I'm more and more convinced that I'm a total masochist. But it's Semur to the rescue as just when I need it the most it brings me a fantastic diversion from all things connected to moving. Every year at the end of May this sleepy town bursts into life with a vengeance with *Les Fêtes Médiévales du Roi Chaussé*, and I've never seen anything like it. The locals go all-out for this festival and it's the most fun I've ever seen a whole town having at once.

But what re-creation of ancient France would be complete without reminders of the bubonic plague? Enter *Les Gueux*, a group of dedicated locals who are devoted to being authentically disgusting.

They go about the streets, yelling, harassing the crowds, subjecting each other to various instruments of torment and sometimes throwing eggs and smelly cheese at folks. Anyway, I know something about medieval torture myself. I spent Saturday at Ikea.

STILL MIDDLE AGED

I was born and raised to this alarming height in St. John's or, as we like to say back home, "town"—famous for fog, a neighbourhood called the Gut, Ches's Fish and Chips and the longest continuously running sporting event in North America, the Royal St. John's Regatta, which is definitely impressive. But it pales in comparison with the oldest horse race in France. Right on the heels, or in this case the hooves, of the medieval festival, comes the *Fête de la Bague*, right here in my little *ville*. Since 1639 they've been at this, 1639!

Paris may indeed be mired in dog *merde*, requiring one to carefully watch every step, but in horse-infested Semur last night a deep inhale would've been warning enough. It's a big event here with the streets filled to capacity with people from all over France. There are hundreds of stalls selling the usual type of market fare but also ones offering the somewhat unexpected. I suppose no medieval horse race would be complete without these ...

Oh, now this is right up my alley. Screw finding a hairstylist (still no luck on that front), all I need is a couple of these and I'm good to go. And speaking of manes ...

These enormous beasts are run in the nod to history race. They charge down a two-kilometre esplanade lined with ancient chestnut trees that has been the course for 373 races. But it's the second race that is truly fierce.

They run so close to the sidelines that you can feel their heat as they zoom past. Absolutely breathtaking. All this majesty and a successful haggle on a very fine linen shirt at one of the stalls, *pas mal*. But I've got my own race to run. Tomorrow is Fête de Sign A Lease In A Foreign Country. "And they're off! As we head into the homestretch, it's Rusty on the inside with Giraffe pulling up the rear ..."

JUNE

A New Lease
on Life

They say you can't teach an old dog new tricks, but this old bitch has been fetching and rolling over like there's no tomorrow. While the language study has been all but abandoned due to *maison* madness, I'm making up for it in knowledge of the complexities of French tenancy. I'm a woman who has signed on the dotted lines. Now I say lines because there were many. I've bought many houses in the past, two before I even met Neil, and I can safely say that I've never been asked for my autograph as much as for sealing the deal on the housette. The lease itself was 60 pages in length, and the diagnostic report, as in the house is not suffering from termitis infestationus, was even longer. Renting a house is quite official here, done at the office of the local *notaire*, a debonair gentleman straight out of a French film. Surrounded by his antiques and elaborate mouldings, he explained the lease line by line. Unfortunately, this little scene was sorely lacking in subtitles. I underestimated how much smiling is involved in pretending to understand page after page of French legalese. My face was frozen into The Joker position for the rest of the day and still hurts.

It was all considerably nerve-wracking, but we signed a standard French contract that seems to favour the rights of the tenants considerably. Of course for all I know there may very well be a clause in that book they call a lease requiring naked chicken dancing on the notaire's desk—me, not him. He hasn't called to schedule that yet so I think I'm in the clear. While I'd rather have my scalp waxed than do the drama of yet another house set-up, I am excited about having a place of my own again. The down side is the loss of freedom from possessions. For one brief moment in time I was weighed down by nothing more than a mattress, a few boxes and a bunch of dated but lengthy clothes. Now, I will once again own things necessitating large trucks and burly butt-crack-revealing movers.

This time, I'm not even going to bother with emphatic statements about how I'm never doing this again. Who'd believe me? Besides, there's too much to do. While the previous tenants were kind enough to sell us the cupboard doors, they did take all the light fixtures, *c'est normal* around these parts, another thing to add to the ever-growing list. And then there's that little issue of the toxic fumes emanating from the newly replaced and all-important second toilet. What odds I say, I'll find the time. It's not like I'm scheduled to conduct Middle East peace talks next week. I mean really, what am I on about? It's not like I have a full-time job across the Atlantic. I don't have to do all the phone calls and letter writing, lease translation and heavy lifting now do I? No, those tasks fall to someone I know who has the patience of a saint, a mind like a steel trap and the heart of a happy child. The bulging biceps are just a bonus.

SURPRISE PARTY

Well, it's one for the books and can only be recorded in the Wild and Wonderful Things About a French Life section. Early last week, one of our landlords called to say that they wanted to come down from Paris to check up on a few things before we moved in. Being overrun with thrilling things to do like figuring out if we'd brought a cheese grater from Canada, I casually asked him if he needed us there. He did, we had the keys. Fine, quick dash up there at eleven, *bonjour*, toilet smells, *merci, au revoir* and then back to buying dishes. Well, clearly some conspiring went on in Paris because at about 10:30 one of the other landlords left a voicemail saying they wouldn't be able to make it until about noon. They'd decided to meet up with some friends to have a picnic on this beautiful day and would we like to join them? At first I thought, oh now a Frenchy picnic, *avec plaisir*! But with so much to do and Neil's work schedule ramping up, we decided that we'd better get our business done quickly and let everybody resume their regularly scheduled programs.

We were all ready to give them a quick rundown of the issue at hand, or in this case at arse, but as they arrived I was quite distracted by the number of people approaching the house and all the bags they had with them. As it turned out, our landlords had invited their friends who'd heard the many tales of the renovation of the little house in Semur but never had a chance to see it. What was becoming apparent was that their picnic was at our house. And before I could say *pardonnez-moi*, one Parisian after another was coming through the door and within minutes the housette was at full capacity. They were all touring the house, congratulating their friends on their successful venture while the kids ran up and down the stairs and skipped rope on the terrace. Neil and I were completely dazed, making all sorts of peculiar faces at each other, desperately attempting to decipher the etiquette of this one. It all happened so fast that there was nothing to do but sit back and enjoy the show.

From their bags they pulled fresh *baguettes* and cheeses, a tomato tarte, roasted turkey, *charcuterie* complete with mini cutting boards, fresh fruit, glasses, a corkscrew and bottles of very fine wine. They spread it all out on the sunny terrace and settled in. They were all charming, fascinating people and so very encouraging about our new place. They even offered to put us up on our next visit to Paris. After a couple of hours they packed it all up, thanked us for having them, double kissed all around and as quickly as they'd all appeared, whoosh. They were off. It was the best party we never had.

Two things I've learned from this caper: one, always shower and change out of your sweatpants before leaving your house for any reason, and two, this notion of Parisians as standoffish is simply not true. From what I've seen they're full of warmth and hospitality. You just have to be ready for them to spring it on you.

TOUR DE FRANCIS

You know it's funny how things work out in this life. When we came to Semur on vacation last year, on our very first walk through town, we stumbled upon a house that literally left me speechless, no easy feat.

I had Neil take a picture of me pretending to open the gate and we bolted off in case the owner saw us. Since then it has never once failed to lift my spirits. But imagine my spirits when I discovered that it is the home of our friend Francis. Now I have the pleasure of seeing it whenever I like, up-close and personal.

Incroyable indeed. I feel incredibly fortunate to be invited to this magical place and to know the sweet man who lovingly cares for it. He is a warm and gentle soul who makes me laugh every time I see him. He also happens to makes a glorious *tarte tatin*. When Francis was a boy in the north of France, he and his family arrived home one day to find German soldiers occupying their house. They spent much of World War II living in their attic. How wonderful it must be that so many of his days have now been spent here. Of course I'm not the only person who loves *chez* Francis and each year he opens his doors to Semur for the *Jardins et Santé* tour, a charity that recognizes the healing powers of a beautiful garden. And as a person who was a doctor in another life, I prescribe this place for whatever ails you.

SERVICE
WITH A SOURIRE

It was a big day over at the housette: appliance delivery. Now I'm no stranger to this melodrama. We've had to do it for every house we've ever had and it never fails to elicit the pleasure of say … a root canal. We've had it all, stoves arriving smashed, Grand Canyonesque gouges in newly sanded floors but the one that really put me over the edge took place just before we left Canada.

Just days after finalizing the sale agreement of our house, our eight-month-old dishwasher went on the fritz and I was desperate to get it sorted for the new owners. I was dealing with a company, which out of respect shall remain nameless, Sears. The first guy said he'd fixed it. He lied. The second guy said it needed a part conveniently located in Edmonton. The third guy forgot the part and the fourth guy, technically the fifth after a no show, finally solved it but not without an earful from me. It was the famous eight-hour delivery window that especially annoyed me because on two of the five occasions I had to take a whole day off work. I tried politely explaining to him how difficult it was for me to get away from the hospital. I asked him to imagine how ridiculous I felt asking my busy colleague to cover me so I could wait all day for a dishwasher part. He was indifferent and I was enraged. I knew it had gone off the rails when I was reduced to a sarcastic tirade that suggested any disaster at the hospital that day would be all his fault. And then, just to really bring it home, I widened my eyes and lowered my voice, "Gee, I hope no one dies." I felt badly until he offered me his considered response to my rant, "Well, I'm working too you know." A stunning example of both punctuality and logic in very short supply.

Now cut to a housette in France. The van from the local appliance store pulled up at two o'clock, curiously enough exactly when they said they were coming. They carefully unpacked and installed all the gear, programmed the TV and then gave us an incredibly detailed demonstration of how to use everything. Okay, in ridiculously rapid French made all the more terrifying by a thick Burgundy accent, but still. The guys knew every single thing about all the machines despite them being different brands. They apologized profusely because the dryer was delayed and would have to be delivered in a few days time, if that was satisfactory for us. Then they packed up all the boxes and asked if we would like them to cart away all the other boxes we had lying around. And that's the game: France 1, Canada 0. I'm not talking any one store down. I got equally crappy service from the cable and phone companies in Canada. But after this impressive display, it would be hard to go back. It was all so civilized, and I'm all about being civil. So Sears, if you would be so kind, bite me.

How I See It

Only seven more sleeps until I strip down, dive into a vat of olive oil and squeeze myself into the housette. If there's a better way to fit me in I'm all ears. Actually, I'm all legs, hence the problem. So far it's going relatively well I'd say, the key word being relatively. Sometimes I think I'm a person so mired in egotistical fantasy, so sure that I am indeed the centre of the universe, that when evidence to the contrary presents itself I'm actually insulted. How dare reality interfere with my plans. I'd convinced myself that all I had to do was pack a few suitcases, drive 45 seconds to my new home, unpack a few suitcases, locate the corkscrew and wait to be handed the chilled nectar of the grapes.

Not so. Neil's work schedule is so heavy right now that things have gone from hectic to hellish. It's all a bunch of silly things to do but things that are incredibly time consuming and frustrating here in rural France. Every time I get one thing settled and solved, something else falls out of line. Of course, in my narrow self-serving view, no one else would possibly need a van on my moving day. Well, apparently everyone and their *chien* needs a truck that day. So we have to drive an hour in one direction to get a van, drive an hour and a half in the other direction to pick up

a sofa at Ikea (where I see that we now have our own designated parking spot) then back to the house on the river to pack up the rest of our crap. Just to add a little sparkle to the situation, some hooligans decided it would be a great idea to steal all the sewer grates and toss them in the river, Fast Times At Semur High. So there is now a big hole at the top of our driveway and the prospect of getting a van down to the door is rather dim. We'll have to haul everything to a nearby parking lot, "we" meaning Neil and our new friend Steve, who has graciously offered to help for the promise of cold beer.

Still, progress is being made. The TV and Internet are all set up, the golf clubs are tucked away and the cooking utensils are all unpacked and hanging from a little steel bar above the cook top. I sense a priority trend here. I was unpacking a few boxes of clothes over there this evening and I allowed myself to be overcome with that dread I experience every time we change abodes, that old familiar "this place will never be ready" foolishness. So I took a break from the toil and stepped out into the garden for some perspective.

I saw that this place has been long ready without any interference from me and that accepting any reality is easy. I just have to change my point of view.

THE HEAT
OF THE MOMENT

I am, as they say here in France, *installée*. Yes, installed like a towering major appliance and so far I fit just fine. I've only hit my head twice getting out of bed and I know from long experience that could happen to me just about anywhere. Poor Neil is exhausted from all the driving and lifting and hauling and dragging. As for me, never underestimate how draining nagging a man day and night can be. I'm all in, a veritable victim of the move. But so far it's been worth it. I already feel at home in this little house, maybe more so than any other place I've lived. Of course the France factor helps matters considerably.

At this very moment I can hear the church bells ringing and just beyond the stone wall and the lilac trees comes the high sweet voice of the child next door who just happens to speak perfect French—bastard. The sun is shining, the birds are singing and in case it sounds like I'm about to break out the tambourine and start singing *Kumbaya*, there's a nest of bees in one wall of our garden, giant red-arsed bees the size of birds that I have no idea what to do about. And so far two big lizards have dropped in to say hello. Lizards. Plus, we're fully engaged in a battle with an online furniture company. They think it's perfectly acceptable to keep our money for a dresser that was never delivered. Oddly enough, we disagree. I don't have a desk yet so giraffe headquarters has been reduced to a corner of the dining table and a basket in the corner under a giant spider web. And let me see, what else? Oh yes, it's 46 degrees outside. It's like living in Saudi Arabia only I'm allowed to drive. Okay, my husband has forbidden me to drive a standard in his presence, but that's not the same thing at all. At least we've each lost a good five pounds in sweat.

For now, I am here in my little French house and it seems that all is right in my world. I look at my husband and see a man who is completely content and having the time of his life. Not surprising for someone who regards a bowl of ice cream the same way one would a winning lottery ticket. It's not possible to describe how hard he's worked to make all this happen. Sometimes I wonder if he really knows how much it all means to me. I suppose I should shower him with kisses, massage his feet, tell him how wonderful he is and express my unending gratitude. And I will, just as soon as he finishes making my lunch.

JULY

BURIED TREASURE

It's Christmas in July here at the housette. After almost a year in storage and quite aptly on Canada Day, remnants of a past life are slowly making their appearance one by one as we sift through the boxes lovingly dumped in the street so long ago. I'm greatly amused by these cartons of things so necessary that they had to be shipped across a vast sea. And while I'm still scratching my head about the one white towel, there were other discoveries that offered concrete proof that I am indeed a genius.

My beloved buddha statue that I've had for too many years to count. Objectively worthless but subjectively priceless. It was a joyful moment to feel the weight of it in my hand once again. Then we unwrapped this …

Our painting by Canadian artist Shelley Mansel, my Christmas gift to Neil many years ago. No photo could ever do it justice. It's a little piece of home which, when you're a squillion miles away, can be very comforting. And thinking of home, this next treasure reminds us that we are both creatures of the sea, one of the few things missing from our landlocked life here in Burgundy.

It's a huge four-foot by four-foot canvas created by Nova Scotia artist Sara MacCulloch. It's called *Beach* and if I stand in front of it long enough I can almost hear the seagulls. I'd forgotten the impact it has on me so I'm grateful we went through the trouble and expense to bring it. Then I found something really interesting.

My meditation bench, a gift from my generous brother-in-law Scott. For some reason it doesn't seem to have much effect unless I physically plant my arse on it. I just have to make sure it doesn't become a handy place for drying bras. Now I know things might actually be immaterial, but every now and then there are connections to objects that cannot be denied. These seemingly inconsequential objects remind me of where I came from. They somehow define the road that led me here and today they feel important. But the most important thing I own was found hidden under a mountain of cardboard and bubble tape. A sweaty, surly redhead, Dirty Neil, who took one look at me and said, "Just try and ask me to lift one more thing. Go ahead bitch, make my day."

Ma Jolie Housette

When I opened my eyes this morning in my bed tightly wedged under the sharply slanted ceiling, the first thing I saw was the wall of Semur stone located only inches from my head. At first I had my doubts about sleeping in such a tight space but I think a reminder of where I am, the moment I wake up, is a perfect way to start any day. I rolled over and examined the maze of rough wooden beams and thick pegs that hold the housette together and I marveled at the handmade nature of it all. Later, as I sat at our flea market table for breakfast and looked around our new home, the thought that came to mind was that it certainly isn't going to make the next issue of Architectural Digest. But that's the beauty of it. For me, the charm of this house is less about what I like …

And more about what I don't like. If I had come to see this house with the intention of buying it, I would have looked right past the stone walls and beamed ceilings, the ancient stone mantle and the pretty blue doors. I would have seen only the things that needed to be "fixed," like the distasteful (to me anyway) floor tiles. Neil, a skilled plasterer and painter, would have repaired every less than perfectly smooth surface and coated the white walls with a better shade of white. Spa inspired bathrooms are our specialty, so we would've devised a complicated and no doubt expensive strategy to disguise the hideous boiler mounted on the bathroom wall.

Instead, we wisely accepted the housette as it came. As for clever strategies, the fireplace (sadly, not a working one) was converted into the wine storage area. For once I chose function over form. I decided that easy access to wine at all times was a distinct priority, no matter how offensive to my design sensibilities. The only other option was the cave, which would have required me to actually get up off my arse and go outside to get it, so the fireplace it was. I also came to another critical conclusion. The world's smallest kitchen is only big enough for one person, and I nominate Neil.

In our old life, we were so fuelled by the pursuit of the impeccably designed house that we sometimes lost sight of what it means to make a home. We've lived in so many different houses, even a few truly luxurious ones, but looking back I didn't really have much time to enjoy them. This little house has caused me to notice something, to notice everything in fact. Now I have plenty of time to take a good look around me and see the beauty in the everyday things that make up my every day.

Of course it was like it at first sight but even after just a few days here I'm in love. A few more nights together and I think the housette and I could live happily ever after, boiler and all.

THE EYE OF
THE BEHOLDER

A wise woman once said, "Beauty's where you find it." Of course I am referring to the greatest philosopher of our time, Madonna, who had the wisdom to finish it off with, "Not just where you bump and grind it." I've always been able to look at things that are shabby and worn and see them in my mind's eye, remodeled and reborn, which might explain a few interesting relationships in my past but I'm getting off track.

I remain *sans* desk so I doodle away on my laptop while sitting at the dining table located dangerously close to the kitchen, the perfect storm for creating body parts that will need some remodeling. In between *bonbons* and emails I find myself staring out the window and there it is every time.

Sure, it's seen better days, but I look at it, close my eyes and the transformation immediately materializes in my mind. I see the door and windows painted that lovely shade of pale blue-grey so often seen in these parts. I see clay flowerpots on the windowsills overflowing with bright pansies and geraniums. I can even see the soft linen curtains billowing from the open window while the sound of a scratchy French record drifts across the breeze. I spend far too much time staring at this rough diamond, redoing it over and over, when really I should be spending a bit more time looking at my very own eyesore.

The inside of our new home needs no changing, apart from the addition of a servant wing, so I shall have to turn my Obsessive Change Disorder outward. It's already started but as anyone can see, it still needs some attention. We've done plenty of gardens before, once a huge Japanese garden with an elaborate waterfall, but I suspect ornamental grasses and dwarf maple trees won't do here. No, here I see lavender and roses along the low stone wall, huge white hydrangeas in the back corner and ivy-covered walls. I close my eyes and I can see a clematis snaking up the stone wall behind a small park bench that sits on pale gravel, a little piece of French heaven. Neil sees tomato plants and basil, a barbecue and lounge chair, a little piece of husband heaven. The problem is, I want it done yesterday. How hard could it be to metamorphose this mess to its maximum potential (a question I typically ask myself as I enter a gym)? I asked Neil to come and look at it with me, to stand in the middle of the weeds and nettles and close his eyes to conjure up a mental image of it all taking shape. My vision featured a sweaty, sunburned, swearing redheaded man digging and planting to save his life. For some reason, he couldn't see that at all.

PARADISE FOUND

I slaved and I toiled. I reaped and I sowed. I tilled and I filled. And like magic, this appeared …

Mon petit jardin. When I said I toiled and all that, what I meant was that I called a guy named Sebastien who came and did it in a day and for dirt-cheap. I'm so happy to finally have my own little French garden but truthfully it scares me a little. In my old life, finishing a garden was always somehow the cue to put the For Sale sign on the lawn. Dear demons of moving and chaos: please let me have this one for a while. I'll give up swearing. I'll learn the French conditional tense. I'll even consider (I said consider) getting an actual job. Anything, just as long as I don't have to move again anytime soon.

I love the bench the most. I sit there with my cup of tea or glass of wine and I admire the terraced gardens, ancient red tiled roofs and the medieval church as its bells echo across the river every hour, as if I really ever need to know what time it is. And I love the pale gravel, so Frenchy with the added

bonus of no need for mowing. Obviously any garden is never as lovely as it will be next year, but I think it's a good start. It still needs something, like a fountain or a statue. Or maybe just a big old rooster like the one I found today sound asleep in his new lounge chair. Oh god love him, I'm not sure I've ever seen Neil look so peaceful. As I gazed upon my sleeping beauty I thought, this moment calls for quiet reflection. This moment calls for serene contemplation. This moment calls for a bucket of ice water.

The Year of Lounging Dangerously

Last week, our blue bubble car was checked into the garage for some TLC and it stayed there for two days. I didn't even notice it was gone which got my old noodle cooking. A year ago, this insignificant event would have sent me into an out-and-out tailspin. I used to have to book car service months in advance to fit it into my hectic schedule and, thanks be to Acura, I never had a breakdown, not a vehicular one anyway. Small things, big things, everything actually, revolved around my all-consuming job. What a difference a year makes. In fact, it was exactly one year ago today that I woke, unassisted by a jarring alarm clock, to face to my first day of unemployment. Twelve months and 3000 *croissants* later, here I am, a person I often don't recognize. And I don't mean all the times I'm frightened half to death by that grey-haired woman in the mirror.

So two things on this very fine day. First, reflection, on how quickly time is passing and how extraordinarily fortunate I've been to experience this past year which leads me to the second, gratitude. People often ask each other what's the best gift they've ever gotten? For sure I've received many a fine *cadeau* in my day, but now I don't even have to think about my answer: "One time my husband gave me a year off." I know I make fun of him because it's just so easy, but all jokes aside, not a day has gone by in the last year when I don't fully understand just what he's given me. He is an uncommonly beautiful person, he is love in its purest form, and he is my heart.

Anyway, enough about that fool, it's all about me. Who knows what the next year will bring? Really, can we ever predict what even the next moment in time will bring? And while it's wonderful to spend all my time sipping French wine and complaining to my husband that dinner is late, there's always the risk of becoming too settled in a state of repose and re- laxation with no way out. But I had my big girl pants on when I came into this and hopefully I'll be wearing the same pants if the *merde* hits the fan. I still have a little more down time left before I have to figure it all out. My work will be to keep doing what I've been doing and quietly consider my options. It's a dangerous job, but somebody has to do it.

OH. MY. GUEUX.

This little town continues to reveal itself to me and bring me wonders I could never have imagined. Once again medieval is the theme *du jour* and this past weekend *les Semurois* were in fine form.

For days I'd been watching people down by the river preparing for some unknown event. Then yesterday morning, I saw that our street was blocked off with big strapping *gendarmes* all about, so we wandered down the hill to see what was going on. Holy mackerel! The place was an absolute mardi gras. The *Lessive Des Gueux* was in full swing, a festival celebrating "hygiene" rituals from the Dark Ages. Now medieval and cleanliness are not words that naturally occur together in my mind and I knew that this was going to get smelly. With great fanfare, the most disgusting souls in France descended an ancient staircase to greet their many fans.

All Hail the Queen of Filth ...

And the Princess of Pestilence ...

Any woman who comes this close while cackling, "A kiss for the fish?" is a kindred spirit in my view. She reminded me so much of my beloved homeland, where we too ask anyone who wants to become an honorary member of our fair society to make out with a dead fish. But this beauty was tame in comparison to this "lady"...

In her raised hand is a piece of half-rotted fish that she's about to let fly, as is the tradition. I had to duck into a fellow foreigner's house to avoid a wet slimy slap on the head, although several pieces managed to find their way through the open windows. But I have to give the French their due, what exactly are they heaving about? Salmon. Thick filets fit for a delicate sauce and a bottle of chilled Chablis. No kippers will do for this crowd.

So, while the town was being fish bombed, the *Gueux* stormed the river.

Clearly, antibiotics should be handed out by the bucket load for this activity. It's hard to describe the energy and excitement of this day. Everyone was united in spirit and having the time of their lives including us. The festivities went on late into the night, and what a show they put together. They performed an elaborate re-enactment of peasant life with feudal lords, armour clad knights, huge, Xena-like warrior princesses led by the leather-clad Eczema, all narrated by a booming voice from the sky. It was hilarious, which I knew only because Elodie patiently translated for me. Under the bright moon and stars, people juggled torches and danced to music from the Middle Ages as red smoke billowed around the ancient ramparts.

The night ended with a stunning fireworks display while the *Gueux* and all the townspeople sang an ancient Burgundian song, a tradition at any event here whether it's a festival like this one or a feisty handball tournament. It's a song with elaborate hand movements and complicated clapping and is just one of the many things I have to learn if I want to really fit in here. In fact, I'm going to get started on next year's festival right now. As soon as Neil comes out of that office, I'm going to haul a piece of cod out of the freezer and whack him in the head with it. Cultural assimilation is a very high priority for me.

There's No Place Like Home

We've made friends with a couple here who live an enviable life. They met in Hong Kong, were married in South Africa and then embarked on a journey of epic proportions moving from country to country on a whim. They would find work wherever they went and were so successful in doing so that they now have a life that allows them to live half time on the coast of Spain and half time by the river here in Semur. They spend their days meandering about France led entirely by their appetites for the finer things in life. They travel all around this great land in search of the best restaurants and hotels. If I didn't like them so much, I'd hate them. She sends me web links to all the places they visit, and for sure these two really know how to roll in style.

Moi? Not so much. Oh I've been to a few places: Beaune, Dijon, Chablis and a few other wine villages, but for the most part these days I stay put. What with Neil's busy schedule, setting up the housette and a limited budget, it's what's on my plate at the moment. But I can't say it's a bad deal this. Every day for me is a Michelin three star experience. I get up when I feel like it and, beyond laundry and the odd toilet scrub, my time is my own. I have delicious meals served to me by a man who could be on the cover of Scottish GQ. I drink exquisite wine for *centimes* a glass and I meet intriguing people from all over the world every day. Plus, why would I need to go anywhere else when every time I leave my house the first thing I lay eyes on is this ...

Never mind the rest of the country, the only travelling I want to do is over the wall to see what's hidden behind that green door. Someday, maybe I'll see all of France, but for now the yellow brick road ends here.

MODEL OF RESTRAINT

You know the more things change, the more they stay the same. Take Sundays. A new life in France was no reason for me not to spend a grey afternoon watching *The Fugitive* while eating dry cereal out of the box. That is, until I got a call from my husband out on a walk saying he'd landed smack in the middle of a *vide grenier* in the centre of town. Now this was worth abandoning the couch for. *Vide grenier* means empty attic and, despite the moratorium on spending and acquisition, I just had to see if one country's junk is another woman's treasure. Basically, it's a big community wide garage sale, speaking of which I passed a garage on the way that I wish was for sale …

But really, where would I put it? Unfortunately, there's nothing quite like stall after stall of things you don't need to bring on a serious case of the "I wants." The problem over here is that even the stuff people are trying to get rid of sends me swooning. I want these chairs …

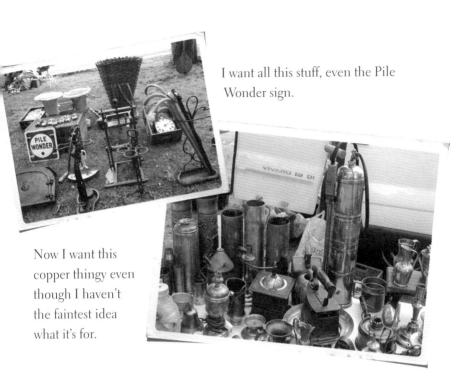

I want all this stuff, even the Pile Wonder sign.

Now I want this copper thingy even though I haven't the faintest idea what it's for.

And I want all three of these.

Regardless of my desire, I was profoundly disciplined and well-behaved. I didn't buy one thing because, as everyone knows, I am a solid and sensible human being. And it wasn't even that difficult. Ten, maybe fifteen reminders from my wise husband that we had neither space nor need for such bric-a-brac was all it took. Although I did come really close on this one …

And I was convinced that, no matter what the cost, I just had to have it, until I remembered … I have one at home exactly like it.

RESTRAINT, MY ASS

Okay, I might not have told the whole story about my afternoon at the Semur *vide grenier*. Those who know me were likely suspicious when I said that a rummage sale would be enough to drag me away from an afternoon with Tommy Lee Jones. I left out something Neil said to me on the phone that had me sprinting up the stairs, one leg already out of the sweatpants that have taken root to me. It seems that a man need only utter one word to get me undressed: donkeys. I love donkeys. We see them around here all the time but always from a speeding car, so when he called and said there were dozens of donkeys in the middle of Semur, I was off like a shot. As expected there were donkeys at work pulling gleeful children around in wooden carts. But the surprise was that the rest of these adorable creatures were for sale! Now, is this the time to talk about fiscal responsibility or space constraints when a donkey or *un ane* (literally translated, an ass) named Tulipe was looking for a good home?

Or what about this one, who reminded me so much of myself that I found it hard to believe that Neil didn't agree we could pass her off as our progeny?

But my favourite of the lot was this little guy. So poised, so agile, so refined and dignified.

I really, really wanted one. But Neil just wouldn't hear of it, he of the great austerity and all that. He just didn't understand that this was not the time to focus on things as petty as money. I mean what woman in her right mind wouldn't break the bank for a new ass?

AUGUST

Meeting
of the Minds

Now that I'm all set up housette-wise, there's really no excuse. I have all the tools at my disposal, three dictionaries, two grammar books, comprehensive conjugation texts, CDs and of course, the ultimate language acquisition strategy—access to an entire population that speaks nothing but the language I'm meant to be learning. But over the last six weeks or so I've let the language study fall so far to the wayside that I've forgotten half of what I've learned. No excuses, but plenty of obvious reasons. Ah, nothing quite like the word obvious to spring a recovering psychiatrist into action. Perhaps there are darker, more sinister, dare I say, unconscious forces at work here. There's only one way to sort this one out. To the Couch.

Retired me: "I must learn to speak French and I want to, I really do."

Dr. me: "Hmm. And yet all I've seen you do today is scarf down enough pastry to choke a pig."

Retired me: "Doc, a girl's gotta eat right? Look, I'm old, well old-ish. I'm lazy. And learning a new language is way more romantic in theory than in practice. It's really hard. Doctor, you just don't understand."

Dr. me: "I understand very well that you've perfected the art of whining and dining. Now here's what else I understand, there's a poor red-headed man sitting at his desk deciphering international tax statutes, in French I might add, to avoid white-collar prison, while a grey-haired woman lounges on the terrace, a Kindle in one hand and a Mai Tai in the other."

Retired me: "Yes, but I think he likes doing everything. I suspect it makes him feel manly and superior and all that. What are you trying to get at, exactly?"

Dr. me: "Well, it's entirely possible that you are avoiding French study so you don't actually have to do anything, so things get magically taken care of without any effort on your part. You know, as a way to escape responsibility for anything."

Retired me: "All right, all right, you might be on to something there. I did hear that you were the best psychiatrist in the world, but I don't know, just once couldn't a cigar just be a cigar? Maybe I'm not cut out for a new language in my state of advanced decrepitude."

Dr. me: "Nonsense. Look at you, why I've never seen a 43-year-old woman of such staggering youthfulness. I mean why you're not the new face of Lancôme here in France is beyond me, but I'm going off track. Remember the other day when your husband presented a bunch of papers for you to sign?"

Retired me: "You mean the driver's licence stuff?"

Dr. me: "Exactly. Somehow this man discovered that France would grant you a driver's licence without having to take a driver's test but only if 25 pages of documents were submitted before a certain date. How he knew this you had no idea, but like everything else he took care of it and all you had to do was sign your name. How does that make you feel?"

Retired me: "Smart. I'm a genius for marrying him."

Dr. me: "Hmm. Interesting. So as long as you avoid French, he'll have to continue to do everything and you can just smile, play dumb and all will be well. How does that make you feel?"

Retired me: "Downright crafty. I have to tell you Doc, the evidence for this I'm-a-genius theory is piling up."

Dr. me: "I think you're not being true to yourself here. I think you might be a little worried that you're not carrying your weight, that maybe you're even taking advantage of his kindness, unconsciously of course."

Retired me: "What is it with you shrinks and this unconscious business? I wish you were unconscious. Okay, okay. I see what you're saying, learn French or be dependent forever. *Merde* or get off the pot. Oh, you are good."

Dr. me: " Yes I know. I think you've made some real progress today but I see that our time is up."

Retired me: "Great, I feel better already. Send my husband the bill."

QUESTIONS AND ANSWERS

Most days I don't give this charmed life a second thought. I roll out of bed at the crack of noon and do whatever comes naturally. It's become routine and mindless and thoroughly effortless. Life just moves along. But because

I am still a recovering psychiatrist I remain somewhat prone to over-thinking with a slight tendency toward endless self-evaluation. Every now and then I'm overwhelmed with what I've done with my life and it comes over me like a wave. It could be hormonal or it could be that I realize what I've given up and what I've left behind—friends and family to sit and chat with over a drawn out meal on a warm summer evening, the people I loved working with, financial independence, sour cream.

The other day as we were driving along a quiet country road, with no warning whatsoever the mind game began. Do you know that you haven't had a haircut since January or set foot in a gym in almost a year? Do you realize that your Canadian residency will lapse in less than two months? You do understand that you have not one job prospect in the foreseeable future, right? (Heart rate rising, skin cold and clammy). I mean what in god's name are you doing here, woman? And then, in the middle of my internal interrogation, France answered me with a whisper, "Stop the car and get out. Stop thinking for a minute and look at me."

"Step back, quiet your mind and be still."

"Now, step back a little more and you'll understand what you are doing here."

"Tell me, right now, in this moment, what else is there to know?" And I knew France was right.

GLOBAL VILLAGE

Being from St. John's automatically makes me a townie, a self-important individual reputed to regard herself as more cultured and sophisticated than anyone in Newfoundland who isn't from St. John's. For the record, let me say that baymen—people not from St. John's reputed to smell of fish and to rely on all-terrain vehicles for transportation—are the true heart and soul of the Rock, the salt of the earth. Of course I have to say that for fear the Sullivan brothers from Dildo (the real name of a real town in Newfoundland) will show up on my doorstep, ready to beat me to a bloody pulp. This townie vs. bayman issue is not to be taken lightly. Anyway, beyond a lesson in my culture, the point is here I am, glamorous townie, installed in France's version of "around the bay." Now there's no actual bay or fish and chips take-out here, but I can't understand a word people say and there's a big tractor garage at the entrance to town, so it's close. But I'm discovering that being a townie brings you little prestige here.

In this little backwater of Semur, apart from our other worldly friends, we've met American physicists/inventors who clearly have a brain cell or two between them, and just last week there were Danish filmmakers hanging about. There's the Russian artist who left New York City to peacefully paint here in the Burgundy countryside, the luxury hotel executive from Hong Kong and his physician partner from New Zealand, and the café owners from Senegal. Sure we could have the Olympics here next week if we wanted to. I'd be heavily favoured for the gold in nagging and self-recrimination.

Last week, we had drinks with two international journalists from Paris who have a weekend house here. She (an American) covers France for the U.S. and Canada and he (*un Parisien*) works in French news television after stints in Washington and Moscow. We were chatting about the state of the economy and it came out that he knows Christine Lagarde, the first female head of the International Monetary Fund (and a rocking silver fox). We were talking about my endless difficulties with French when he mentioned that UN Secretary General Ban Ki-Moon was learning French and doing quite well with it. How did he know this? Because he knows Ban

Ki-Moon. I thought about breaking out my story of how I met Kathy Bates (a more enchanting woman cannot be found) in a restaurant bathroom one time, but I decided it was a tale for another time. And to top it all off, this week, no more than five doors down the hill, Semur welcomes a famous ultra right wing, misogynistic CNN/FOX news political pundit/freak of a man. Clearly, this peaceful life has rendered me serene and free from judging others. I haven't met him yet, but I've seen him a couple of times now through the scope of my rifle. Oh I'm just kidding. It's a water gun.

It's fascinating to be around this kind of energy and to have the opportunity to learn so much about the world. And here I thought I was coming to a place that might be too "small town" for someone as suave and cosmopolitan as myself. Oh, we townies talk a good game and we think we're big fish in a small sea, but the folks here are the ones casting their nets far and wide.

THE BUCK STOPS HERE

Or I should say the euro. While the world markets shake, rattle and roll and the global economy implodes, here in Semur the value of a dollar is as solid as a rock. I mean what can you get for a dollar these days? A handful of candy? Nope. A coffee? I couldn't even buy the foam on a latte for that.

Almost every day since I've been here I've walked past these magnificent doors and longed to see what treasure was hidden behind them. When out of nowhere a brass plaque appeared announcing daily visits every half-hour, "*Deux billets s'il vous plait*," was the only French I needed to know.

The doors alone were enough to make me bow down to the French as masters of the universe and were well worth the one-euro entry fee, but this is what was behind Door Number 1 …

The house itself was off limits, apparently because there's someone living in it. This is somebody's actual house, as in this is what's waiting for them after a long hard day of … yachting or purchasing fine art.

A sweet teenaged guy who seemed very jazzed by the history of it gave us the tour. He told us how it had been taken back by the people during the Revolution and how Voltaire and his ladylove, the Marquise du Châtelet, hung out here concocting the Age Of Reason.

We walked around the grounds for about half an hour while the kid told us everything there was to know about this spectacular place. How's that for a summer job? It has to be better than flipping burgers, or maybe not. He was a compelling and competent guide, but the whole time he was talking I wondered how much flak he takes for being the town's resident history geek. Poor *garçon*, spending all day watching older women order their bedraggled husbands to pick up the pace on the picture taking. My friend Jill's clever theory is that the *garçon's* family owns the house and while his parents frolic on the Italian Riviera, he whips up that plaque right about the same time he finds that he's depleted the pile of cash left by his parents. He can't show us inside the house because his leather-bikini-clad girlfriend is passed out on the 18th century chaise and his stoner buddies are in the middle of a three-day non-stop Xbox tournament. She may be right. About an hour after we left I saw him sauntering down the cobblestone street looking very impressed with himself, trailing a thick cloud of French cigarette smoke while grooving to the sounds from his super-slick headphones. Cool or not, he's still got a thing or two left to learn. I would've paid him any price he asked.

CHANT, RATTLE
AND ROLL

Before I ran away from the circus, I spent my weekends either working or trying to recover from working to be ready to face the next week of disaster known as crisis psychiatry. I can't count how many times I've worked a 30-plus-hour workday without so much as a 15-minute break. I once did it every three days for several years in a row. I don't miss it. My rambling point is that I now have the time, and more importantly, the energy (a relative term at my stage of greyness) to do the things I want to do. This weekend there was actually too much to choose from: live music at a restaurant in town, more music at a local winery and even more music at a monastery just down the road. I love living in a place where there's a 12th- century abbey next to a Citroën dealership. I'd visited this solemn compound before. Neil and I stumbled upon it one sunny morning a few months ago. On that day we had the entire place to ourselves.

It was so peaceful and serene, completely silent except for a soft recording of monks singing. It was one of those chilling moments when your entire body is one big goose bump. Of course I was not content to have only one chilling moment. Behind the original buildings were several large houses of such staggering architectural beauty that they just had to be seen close-up. In my defense, I was too busy oohing and aahing to see the ridiculously tiny sign that said Private — Not Part of Tour (in French, so double not my fault). I climbed the stairs of the most impressive of the lot and started wiggling the doorknob. I called back to my photographer who, strangely, was no longer by my side. "Neil, Neil, look at me, I'm pretending I live here. Take my picture. Go on, it'll be *fantastique*." It was not. I mean first, who actually owns a monastery and second, who actually lives in one? Apparently, rich French people.

Anyway, normally after I humiliate myself somewhere (pharmacies, any bar on the east coast of Canada) I try my best not to go back to the scene of the crime, but I figured under the cover of darkness no one would be the wiser. It's not every Saturday night that I can witness Gregorian chanting by candlelight at an ancient French monastery, so I took the risk. Now I've taken in a few great shows in my life, Springsteen, Clapton, U2, Aerosmith, The Stones, Bob Dylan, and my sister has experienced everybody else. But we both concede defeat to our mother who wins hands down as she once went to a dance where the music was supplied by Diana Ross and The Supremes. Then, a short time later, she sat bewildered among throngs of screaming women while four lads from Britain sang songs she could hardly hear. I can't top the Beatles, but these monks sure know how to show a girl a good time, and it was a performance I won't soon forget.

The light show was nothing short of spectacular, gravel pathways lit by torches, thousands of white candles everywhere and a dramatically clear night with a luminous full moon and shooting stars. We strolled around the grounds under the brightest blue moonlight I have ever seen until the huge wooden doors opened and the chorus of ancient voices began. I don't know who does the costumes for these guys, but the monks were styling in long white robes that seemed to glow in the soft candlelight. And they must have a killer sound crew because their voices rose to the curved stone ceilings with a clarity and timbre that caused even the flapping bats to settle and listen. Security was a little on the slack side though, as people were allowed to meander freely or sit on the ancient stone staircases and see the show from any angle. Even the kids were enraptured. Our friend Carmel's ten-year-old daughter Lily, tipped her sweet, smiling face forward and in her Irish lilt exclaimed, "It's really good, isn't it?" And it was.

At one point I begged Neil to let fly his best concert whistle but for some reason he wasn't keen, nor was he in favour of me performing my patented concert "whoooooyeeaaahh!" He also wasn't down with me asking the lead singer to sign my chest; does this man know anything about the art of concert attendance? I had heard that the abbey was available for private parties and I couldn't imagine getting my groove on here. I thought I'd be too busy blessing woodland creatures and begging for forgiveness, but now I'm not so sure. We did manage to get backstage access and capture a rare glimpse of the after show party.

I can only imagine the trail of trashed hotel rooms all throughout France not to mention the line of groupies waiting at the back door. But of all the shows I've seen, this one is now in the running to be my all time favourite, even if I didn't get to sit on Neil's shoulders and rip my top off to reveal MONKS ROCK scrawled in black marker across my boobs. Next time.

Smooth Talker

One thing I know for sure is I hit the jackpot in the husband lottery. And while he's perfect for me, that doesn't mean he's perfect. Oh if there's a fence that needs building or a meal that needs cooking, he's your man. But if there's a conversation that needs finessing, I'd have better luck with a plant. I'll be offering a fascinating perspective on the nuances of some Victorian novel and I'll see the clouds pass over his face, a dull faraway look forming in his eyes, and it's at that moment I realize he is clearly not hanging on my every word. At the best of times he's the king of one-word responses and anytime after ten o'clock at night, grunts reign supreme. Of course the silence is often a welcome change from some of his "compliments." I've had this husband for a while now so I should know better than to expect anything different, but ever the optimist, I keep thinking any day now he'll come around. And already there are signs of the turning tide.

Over the last few weeks he's been talking up a storm on exhilarating topics like withholding taxes and transfer pricing, RRSPs, TFSAs, health care affiliation and international incorporation. It seems it's true what they say about reaping what you sow, because the minute he starts in on this stuff I feel my whole body starting to go limp. By the time he gets to a point where he needs a reply from me, I manage to slur out, "Whatever you think is best, my love," before I slide off the chair with my chin on my chest and a line of drool down the side of my face. But today it's occurring to me that it might've been a good idea to pay a little more attention to his sweet nothings. While I've been busy lounging and scrounging, little by little he's been setting up a life for us here and, in doing so, cutting the cord to Canada.

I know my psychiatric colleagues will shake their heads at my tenuous grasp of the obvious but I have a sneaking suspicion that we might be staying in France. I guess my first clue should've been signing a long-term lease and buying major appliances, but denial's not just a river in Egypt, it's a powerful thing. Truth be told, I don't really want to think about anything more complicated than where my next *pain au chocolat* is coming from. So technically it's suppression rather than denial, but I'm retired, so who gives a *merde*? At any rate the fat lady's song is long finished. Very soon we'll have French driver's licences, French health cards and the right to protest in the street about paying exorbitant taxes. Being former Canadians, we'll have that one down in no time.

So maybe I have to remind him how nice I look whenever we go out and maybe he's never going to want to chat late into the night about books and music and films. But when it comes to getting things done no man can top him, and for that I'm eternally grateful. But let's be perfectly clear on who's the real smoothie in this mess. If this turns out to be a disaster it'll be entirely his fault and I know for a fact that no matter how hard he tries, he'll never be able to talk his way out of it.

SEEK AND YE SHALL FIND

Yes, poor Neil. He has to work. He has to do all the things that need doing to build a life here. He has to feed me and deal with me on a 24-hour basis and it's that last one that will finally see him curled in the fetal position on the cold floor, sucking his thumb and begging for salvation. Cry me a river. What about me? I too have had to carry my share of the burden.

While French bureaucracy has taken its toll on him, the King has made the official decree that since we're ready to fake being French we will be staying. I'm well aware of the importance of tax complications and immigration laws, but steady on Your Majesty, the Queen wishes to speak. Earlier I said that if I couldn't find some sour cream I was bailing. Very well, I'm willing to concede defeat on that one. However, it is with great pride and not a shred of humility that I announce my victory over the two most crucial problems impeding my ability to commit to a life here.

Victory Number One: my arse, specifically the future of my arse. I've discovered the holy of holies, a gym. It's small, 20 minutes away, I have to join an *association sportive* and have a *certificat médical* before they let me in the door, but they have a discount for people who are retired or unemployed, so either way I'm saving. Plus, all grey-haired women six feet tall and over actually get paid to go so people have something to point at and laugh. I made that last bit up but the rest is true. Oh the relief when I saw all the leg machines. I joke a lot about my arse, and for sure it's worth a snigger or two, but I need that gym for my bum leg and that's no laughing matter.

Victory Number Two: my head. At long last a razor-wielding hairstylist has been found, right here in Semur. A while back Elodie, *amie* and physiotherapist to the star, mentioned a promising prospect, Cedric. Then a few days later a local woman took my picture for my French driver's licence application—I call it anemic criminal with no lips. I won't show it here because, naturally, it'll be the one plastered all over the news if anything untoward happens to me over here. The photographer had the first funky do I've seen here in town so, poor grammar aside, I weaseled out of her who was responsible: Cedric. I was off like a shot and *voilà*, there he was, totally fabulous, a dachshund in one hand and a razor in the other, my kind of guy.

So now, apart from the whole Miracle Whip issue, as in there isn't any, I have no more excuses, no reasons at all why I can't stay in this strange and wonderful place where somehow I seem to be finding everything I've been looking for. Unless I count being jobless, language-less and generally scared to death. But who's counting?

HOT AND HEAVY

All is not lost on the language acquisition front. The good news is this week I've learned a new word, *la canicule*. The bad news is it means heat wave. It's 40-odd degrees here and the famous Burgundy snails are moving faster than I am these days. I mean it's like hair-plastered-to-your-head, change-your-underpants-three-times-a-day hot.

Our bedroom is actually an attic and all it needs is a few cedar benches and a stocky Scandinavian woman named Grunhilda and we're in the sauna business. I refuse to keep the windows open at night because a woman I know here slept with hers open and woke up with a bat on her face. A bat. On her face. I'd never survive that, nor would Neil if I woke up and saw a bat on his face. I can see the headlines now, Crazed Canadian

"Batwoman" Beats Husband To Death With Alarm Clock. Ah, but there's nothing quite like sweat-soaked sheets, a man who, at the best of times, generates enough heat to keep Alaska toasty and a fear of flying rodents to stoke the fires of romance. One more night of this mess and we'll be divorced or dead. I'm no good for this. By two o'clock in the afternoon I'm like an oil spill, greasy, grimy and toxic to seabirds and husbands. The only thing saving the marriage at this point is I'm too wilted to talk. I can't even open the front door until the sun goes down.

They say we're in for another four or five days of *la canicule* but I guess I shouldn't complain. The dog days of summer will be gone soon enough and I'll be back to wearing long johns to bed and begging that furnace I call my husband to warm those blocks of ice I call my feet. But for now, if he comes within a foot of me never mind the clock, he's getting the hose.

FATHER
FORGIVE THEM

… for they know not what pigs they are. No, I'm not talking about Dominique Strauss-Kahn, the new national obsession of this great nation. Who needs big time porkers when I have small time *cochons* to disgust me?

There I was, traipsing about my little French town looking *très chic* (that might be a stretch, but no sweatpants or orthopedic clogs), with my aviator sunglasses and my new French scarecut, not bothering a soul, a skip in my step and a song in my heart. Up the old stone stairs I climbed when I came upon a gaggle of giggling teenaged girls. They always make me smile, these gorgeous young *femmes* as they pour themselves over the stairs, fiercely exerting their independence with their matching clothes and hairstyles. They stopped pouting and posing long enough for a polite, "*Bonjour, Madame.*" So charming this lot.

Then a turn of a corner and a turn for the worse. Enter *les garçons* of summer, a formidable posse of seven or eight loud, beefy guys of no more than 18 years apiece. Once face to face with them I smiled, said "*Bonjour,*" and waited for permission to pass. Dead silence as I made my way by until one of the snakes hissed, "*Ahh, tu es très jolie,*" followed by peals of laughter. I just assumed they'd met up with one of the girls but when I looked back I realized they were referring to *moi*. Now here's what's wrong with this picture. I'm no French linguist but I know enough to know that I am to be addressed by hooligans I've never met, decades younger than me with "*vous*" not "*tu.*" In this culture of politesse it's incredibly rude and insulting. And after the first boy went over the edge, the lemmings followed with a series of catcalls, clever phrases like "yum yum" and various slurping noises that continued the whole time it took me to get up the stairs.

Now for those thinking these Frenchmen in training were nursing fantasies of an older woman, I can confidently say that they were clearly making fun of me. In fact, they were pointing out how incredibly ridiculous it would be to consider me attractive. I remember the drill all too well from high school. These bozos wouldn't know a compelling woman if she fell on them. Which explains why they were clustered at the top of the stairs while a dozen budding supermodels in various states of undress, literally around the corner, were wasting their mascara and perfume on each other. Instead, these guys thought it a better use of their time to harass some foreign woman old enough to be their mother.

The real problem is that this rude awakening has completely messed with my "this is the friendliest town in France where *merde* like this doesn't happen" delusion. Until now, every single encounter I've had with people here has been remarkably pleasant. Even the people at the bank were uncommonly gracious while refusing to lend me money. The worst part was having to walk silently on amid the taunts. As someone who's always seemed to draw the room's biggest loser (once a guy with two teeth wearing a floor-length leather coat), I'm quite used to having a snappy comeback in response to this kind of thing. But for these morons I had nothing, *rien*.

Oh sure, I could say that I was out of practice or that I saw their lewd adolescent behaviour for what it was: insecurity, angst and a lack of positive role models. Or I could say that I am now enlightened and above what others think of me; that living the simple life has fundamentally changed me into a serene person who feels nothing but compassion for their enemies, someone like Jesus or that little guy from India. The sad truth is I just didn't know the French for, "Oh yeah? Well suck me arse, ya bunch of slimy halfwit swine," until I was home with my dictionary of French insults. Somehow, barrelling up the stairs and screaming that at a bunch of kids two hours after the fact would've been a little light on the femme fatale and a bit heavy on the raving lunatic. Next time, I shall channel my inner messiah, smile, raise my hand in blessing and say, "Father, I ask forgiveness for my young brothers—right after they suck me arse."

ALL IN A
DAY'S WALK

Heat waves and harassing hooligans aside, I love this town. One of the great things about living in France is how the everyday becomes the sublime. Places that I always took for granted in Canada like banks, libraries or city hall because they were, well, boring, take on new meaning here in Semur.

I often start or finish my day here at *Mademoiselle* Elodie's House of Pain.

She calls it physiotherapy, which in French is pronounced sadistic torture. Oh, I'm just teasing, she saves my life three times a week. After Elodie finishes untwisting the pretzel lady, I'm loose enough to promenade home and the first place I see is the *Caisse d'Epargne* also known as a bank.

When the banks look like this they get a certain amount of latitude no matter how arduous the process of seeking mortgage approval. A few more steps and the local library comes into view.

When I am queen of the world (any day now) all libraries will look exactly like this one. In the centre of the courtyard there are benches where I can sit and take it all in, which is convenient because there's not much point of me hanging about inside, not even in the preschool section. Ah, but someday soon I'll proudly check out my first French book, preferably one with lots of pictures and really big print.

Next, I pass through the gates of city hall.

When I first came to France I noticed almost every town had a *Hotel de Ville*, which I thought was the French answer to Holiday Inn. Not so, a *Hotel de Ville* is the administrative hub of town. It's a veritable extension of *La République*, where one seeks permission to live in France from *Monsieur le Maire* himself. The crowd at this one has offered us a level of service that a Howard Johnson's just couldn't touch.

What I love about living here is that a simple walk to the physio clinic is inspiring and beautiful and makes me feel happy all over. Of course, every place in the world has its own beauty and no town is perfect. To be sure, there are parts of Semur that are crumbly, shabby and in need of some serious overhauling, but I've seen my *derrière* today so who am I to talk?

It's Everywhere
I Want to Be

Sometimes my relationship with France can only be described as a hot/cold, love/hate, up-and-down-faster-than-a-whore's-drawers kind of thing. As I amble home through the quiet streets of Semur, I marvel at how uncomplicated my life has become, how unfettered and uncluttered by the daily grind. Oh yes, as long as I don't ever have to speak to anyone, this living in a foreign country is a breeze, a piece of *gâteau*. I often speak too soon.

About twelve years ago some swindler in Guadalajara, Mexico ran up a tab on my Visa of over $7000 without even so much as a *por favor* or *gracias* to me. I called the credit card company, they took care of it all and I went back to conveniently using my card for everything from Chinese food delivery to international trouser purchases. France, however, is not exactly a credit card culture—yet. Our French MasterCards are nothing more than glorified ATM cards and people still write cheques for just about everything here. The point is, yesterday, my Minister of Finance was looking over our monthly statement and found 500 euros of charges that he couldn't make sense of.

Now our mantra here is "can we get by without it?" This is our year of living skinny (arse, please take note of this new policy) and I'm happy to say that apart from the odd book, I've been behaving myself. I mean if I had 500 euros lying around, that gorgeous grey trench coat just begging for a silver-haired owner would be hanging in my closet instead of the boutique window. We'd been *volé*. Bastards. A scam where slippery characters post phony telecom company charges to your account and hope you won't notice. Good thing for us my *monsieur* doesn't miss a trick. Of course this also makes it very hard to sneak in a new pair of shoes. Ah well, no matter, one call does it all, back to pouring the wine. Not so fast, *Madame*, you should know by now that France is hardly the land of instant gratification.

We called the number on the back of the card that really should connect you to dial-a-prayer, as it would have been more helpful. Then we went off to the bank where the cards were cancelled without our permission and no offer of immediate replacements was made. The bank assured us the cancellation was for our protection, as the thieves could be spending more of our money over the weekend. Well they wouldn't get far on our little stash but really, how the hell was this our problem? Oh the Minister was not pleased, especially when we were handed a mountain of forms to fill out. The bank washed their filthy hands of us and directed us to the local police station as the fraudulent charges had to be officially reported. And, *bien sûr*, the station was closed, more paperwork and more fun for another day.

It's an odd setup over here bank wise, and I'm still trying to get used to it. I still have my Canadian Visa card but the practical use of it here is very limited, which is a good thing, at least according to the Minister's Office. But I can't blame France. This goes on everywhere and anywhere but they sure don't make it easy when it does happen here. Yet again a new test of resolve and willingness to accept what it is.

Thieves hacking into your supposedly private bank account: 500 euros. Dealing with French financial bureaucracy: several handfuls of hair and buckets of sweat. Finding new European credit cards: 17 phone and Internet hours. Loving your new life in France warts and all: priceless.

SEPTEMBER

COPS AND ROBBERS

Being an emergency room psychiatrist involves working closely with the police on a daily basis. So for me, no new life would be complete without a visit to the local cop shop. Here France's finest wear pale blue polo shirts with GENDARMERIE printed across the back and cool navy cargo pants tucked into black army boots. They're quite sporty and always look ready for the chase. While the cops in Canada are also ready, willing and able, they sometimes appear a little starchy in their crisply pressed dress shirts and stiff hats.

Anyway, since we were the victims of the most heinous crime of bank card hacking, we went to make an official complaint or *porter pleinte*, as it's known in these parts. The police station here is as unremarkable a building as you can find in France, a modern piece of nothing special. As I walked inside and surveyed the rundown interior, complete with grubby vertical blinds and tired rubber plants, I could've easily been in any station in North America. But then I looked at the wall behind the front desk and saw large marble plaques commemorating the loss of local *gendarmes*. Lost, not in the line of duty, but Killed by the Enemy, 1944 and Deported to Buchenwald, 1942 and then I remembered where I was. Suddenly, this bland precinct seemed historic enough.

We were met by an officer best described as thick: thick hair, thick arms, thick hands, all business. He took our names and birth dates and told us we'd have to wait ten minutes while he went in the back. Suddenly, his voice called from beyond asking us if we had a *femme de menage* to which my husband, too quickly, responded no. I gave him the stink eye reminding him that we do indeed have a cleaning lady—me, which prompted Neil to ask me if I'd stolen our money. I can only assume there's some cleaning lady ring of thieves in Semur. I'll keep it in mind as I reflect on my next career move.

He then invited us into his office for the next stage of the process. We sat, he typed and the *rendez-vous* meandered into a friendly hour-long chat about how we came to be here, police life in Semur and how much I liked their uniforms. "*Bah, non!*" he exclaimed and jumped up to show me all kinds of pictures of the more formal police wear that, and I just had to trust him on this one, was much better. Oh, I love a cop with style. He showed us old posters of Semur from the 1930s, told us about a film we could see showing the town many years ago and explained how and where they work in the area. He told us how he'd taken English and German lessons but didn't get the chance to use his skills much. So, obviously more than just thick, this one.

And then we got to talking about crime. I told him about my recent harassment and, to my surprise, he was quite interested. He asked me to describe the boys, but apparently, "Big and rude with absolutely no empathy for the difficulties of being a middle-aged woman in our society," isn't that useful. Then he turned his computer screen around to show me a mugshot of a menacing youth who may or may not have been one of the offenders. I told him I couldn't be sure and then he said, "He's here in the back, want to take a look at him?" Jaysus god alive, no I don't want to take a look at him. Arrested for wielding a knife and I should stand in front of him, extend a bony finger and triumphantly exclaim, "YES, officer, YES! He's the one who made fun of me in the street and made me feel old!" Like I want to walk around a very small town looking over my shoulder for this jackass for the rest of my days.

Anyway, I've met a lot of great cops in my day and he was by far the most congenial of the lot, a true credit to the French police service: polite, charming and I bet he can kick some major arse when necessary. After we left, we wished we had gotten his name. Another Frenchy factoid: disclosing names isn't often done here, even in official capacities. Officer Friendly wasn't even wearing a nametag. We're still trying to get used to the famous French discretion that requires names to be exchanged only if absolutely necessary. It seems small but it's really hard for two polite Canadians to get a handle on. Not that it matters. He told me if I had any more problems in Semur he'd be happy to help. I know where to find him and if I need him again I'll just call and ask for the good cop. It seems the bad cop works somewhere else.

Open Season

I just love September. It's always been my favourite month. When I was a kid I had an inexplicable fondness for school supplies. Now, while three-ring binders and mechanical pencils still give me a certain thrill, it's more about nature's autumnal majesty. Here in Semur, the days remain hot and sunny but the cool misty mornings and crisp starry evenings make enduring summer heat waves worthwhile. The leaves are in full fall splendour and already I can smell the sweet scent of chestnut fires burning again. It's magic. I know that this will all be too quickly replaced by a long, grey winter, so I'm frantically trying to spend as much time as possible soaking up the pleasures of the season.

Today we woke to a glorious Sunday and decided that we should finally get over to see the *château* in Lantilly, a town just around the corner. For some reason we hadn't managed to drag our pastry-laden arses over there yet, and once we did my suspicion that we are the worst tourists in the history of French tourism was confirmed. The weekend before last was the one weekend a year when all the French *châteaux* are fully open for viewing, free of charge. And what was I doing? I don't even remember, but I'll bet it involved eating. And today we discovered the *château* closest to us was now closed for the season. How can we be this lazy about seeing the wonders of France? While I fully expect such ridiculous behaviour from myself, I was especially disappointed in Neil, who is supposedly perfect in every way.

But the day wasn't a total loss. As we drove home, we passed through a pretty village called Grignon, not far from Semur, where I saw the perfect place for a fall fix. So I grabbed my phone, hopped out of the car and raced down the lane.

It's no French castle, but it is beautiful. Then I turned my back to the lane to have a better look around and capture this vista for my photo collection …

While I was squatting in the driveway, I saw the blue bonnet of our car out of the corner of my eye and I quickly turned to get in. Instead, I turned smack into an elegant gentleman dressed in his Sunday finest and holding a Bible who coincidentally, also has a blue car. I didn't quite catch all that he said to me but "my house" was in there for sure. Holy trespassing, how do I get myself into these situations? Add in a few frayed nerves and my French goes from bad to worse so I knew I wasn't getting out of this one on my own. And where was my beloved? Watching the whole thing unfold from our car at the end of the lane. I fired him a look that said two things: thanks for the warning, dingbat, and get out of the bloody car and come help me. As it turned out, the man wasn't angry at all, merely curious if I was taking pictures for a blog or a book. I guess he's used to the world stopping to admire his home. He was incredibly obliging and said that while he didn't have time right then, we should call on him another day when he would be pleased to give us a tour of the village and its church, which he assured us was *magnifique*.

It always amazes me how eager people are to show off the treasures of this land but then again, look what they have to offer. This time I was just plain lucky. One of these days I'm going to wander too far in the name of pretty pictures and end up face to face with a farmer's rifle. Next time, I'll wait in the car and send Neil in for the shot.

So Near
and Yet So Far

One of the best things about Semur is that it's a mere hour from Paris. And one of the worst things about Semur is that it's a mere hour from Paris. This is when *ma vie en rose* stinks a little. Last week Jerry Seinfeld performed a stand-up routine at a small cabaret club in that city 60 minutes from my door. Sixty minutes by high-speed train that is, it's a six-hour round trip by car. Apparently he did his usual schtick and afterwards held a Q & A session with the audience, an audience of which I was not a member. *Merde.* I love all his good, clean fun that makes me laugh until my face hurts. I've never once seen him perform and this time it was not to be either.

First, tickets to the show: 67 euros times two. Then, train tickets to Paris: 70 euros times two. Then, because there's no train back until the next morning, a hotel room for a minimum of 150 euros, but at that price the lice-infested sheets would be free. So all totaled, at least 425 euros (not including the requisite *pâtisserie* raid) to enjoy an hour of witty observations about pizza crust and laundry. Don't get me wrong, I would have gladly parted with it, but the tickets for the show alone were beyond my budget, and there's the rub.

French funemployment is *fantastique*, it just doesn't pay very well. It's great to have the freedom to do nothing but to anyone thinking about giving it a go, be really prepared to do nothing. All kinds of wonderful things go on up in that Paris place: George Michael concerts, candlelight cello performances in historic chapels, operas, author readings at Shakespeare and Company. Oh why do I torture myself? All this is going on and will continue to go on without me until such time as my name appears on a paycheque. I was more than prepared to forego fancy skin creams and expensive restaurants as the tradeoff for this layabout life, but the rest can take a toll sometimes. How I laugh at myself, she of the quest for simplicity and joy. But I can't have it all, no matter how entitled I think I am.

Now in no way do I slight my husband's hard earned salary, which pays for all the necessities, but without a second income any luxurious extras are out, well, apart from a loungy life in France. In theory, I accept this living skinny business, it's just that my brain and my thighs haven't fully made peace with it yet. We've decided that any extra money found should be saved for travel, one of the main reasons for deciding to settle in this part of France in the first place. We have offers to visit friends in Spain and Vienna and I think experiences like those are worth missing out on smaller things.

I think the key is ignorance. I'll stop looking and I'll never know what I'm missing. And besides, there's plenty of free entertainment right here. Neil has a guitar, a black leather jacket and mirrored shades, so George Michael, eat your heart out. Plus, I have my first French gynecology appointment today and, unless my French improves dramatically in the next hour, I'll need Neil to translate, my own *Seinfeld* episode just waiting to happen. "So, we walked into the gynecologist's office and yadda yadda yadda, Neil ran screaming from the room and I never saw him again."

Real Men Eat Tarte

Not long after we arrived here on our *rue*, I noticed that a house across the street, previously shuttered up tight, was slowly coming to life. Each day the door opened and out came a serious looking fellow of a difficult to say age with a thick grey mustache and beard and sporting a myriad of tattoos. He wore Moroccan leather sandals with soles that curled up over his toes, the kind you see on movie characters riding Arabian horses through the desert while brandishing giant curved swords. In my head he was mysterious, dangerous even. I had all kinds of wild stories attached to him.

Despite my intrigue, as usual, timidity trumped curiosity and I never got beyond a sheepish *bonjour* to him. Then, a few weeks ago, Neil and I were huffing up the hill and there he was, standing in the middle of the street. He offered us a deep and solemn *bonjour* and said, "Jean-Claude." Finally, someone in France opened with a name. He paused and looked at us intensely, "Do you like apples?" Well, of course we like apples. Then he raised a large arm and with a toss of his hand directed us to his truck. Next thing I knew we were bouncing up the road with this enigmatic stranger, in my mind the local mafioso who ferries unsuspecting immigrants to a secret dog fight arena. He stopped in front of a large plot of land full of bushes and trees and got out. Curious indeed. I decided to trail behind the men just in case I had to make a break for it.

The ground was covered with hundreds of apples and the bushes were heavy with blackberries. Suddenly, the formerly stoic Jean-Claude was happily showing us his bounty and then turned to Neil (not to me now, to Neil): "You know these apples make a delicious tarte but don't use the darker ones, they can be a bit sour." And with that they were off into a lengthy discussion about baking. Well, I never.

He offered us the use of his orchard whenever we liked and invited us in for a tour of his office. I was ready for anything, bounty hunter, hired assassin, arms dealer but I settled for the truth: plumber. Then he invited us to join him for an *apéritif*. We walked through his office into his inner sanctum, a large room that is impossible to accurately capture in words. Let's just call it a personal museum. Pistols by the dozen, antique rifles from Afghanistan and Switzerland. Ancient knives, daggers and swords. Animal skins, fossilized shark teeth, giant African masks and statues hand carved from huge trunks of ebony wood. Lacquered Asian armoires, jade figurines and heirloom pocket watches. He also had a vast number of military medals and honours including a Cold War peace commendation signed by Donald Rumsfeld. So much for my dark side theory.

Then he led us down a small flight of stone stairs to a medieval wooden door from which hung a mammoth metal padlock from the 16th century. Behind that door was his true collection, a cave full of wine. A lot of wine. Enough wine to keep a Newfoundland wake swinging for at least 24 hours. He had bottles from as far back as 1915. For us he chose a white wine from 1990, the colour of butterscotch and exquisitely fruity, then an ice-cold champagne, the best I've ever tasted. It could have been the tales of his adventures, the beard and all the African rifles (also could have been the wine), but as the hours slipped by in his exotic chamber, I became more and more convinced that he is actually Ernest Hemingway.

Since then, he has come to our door time and time again with apples and Neil has gone to his door with bowls of hot apple crumble. Next thing you know the two of them will be quilting and going for facials. Last week he returned from his vacation with a treat for us, a jar of dark, aromatic honey from his father-in-law's farm in Corsica. Yesterday yet another basket of apples appeared on my doorstep. And today he handed us a CD by a popular French folk band, signed personally by one of the musicians, "To Neil and Bobbi, *Amitiés*." Now he and his equally charming wife, Jacqueline, are making ready for the long drive to their second home in Morocco. They'll be gone for a month and I miss them already.

He's a splendid example of the intriguing people who have come into our French life; wonderfully compelling characters who seem to have magically sprung to life from the pages of a French screenplay. I suspect it will be an adventure just being his neighbour. This morning I saw him climbing aboard his Mercedes SUV, wearing a black leather fedora adorned with a band of crocodile teeth as well as a python vest, red leather pants and cowboy boots. Oh yes, JC and I will get along just fine.

A Matter of Life and Death

Obviously doctors see their fair share of death, and as a lowly intern I recall a particularly dismal shift. In the course of about 30 hours, I pronounced six people dead, one of whom was an elderly nun. Her fellow sisters were gathered in prayer outside her room when I brought them the news. They smiled, thanked me and went back to their prayers while I dashed off to my next encounter with the grim reaper. I never had much time in those days to stop and ponder the meaning of life or death, it was just part of the busy routine. But now that I am finally living my life to the fullest, I have time to think about life, death and everything in between. And today, as I stumbled upon a small cemetery, I thought about a lot of things.

It was so quiet and peaceful, much like the reaction of those nuns. I suppose in their minds their sister was off to her eternal resting place, that "better

place," which I'm sure they imagined as heaven with St. Peter and a father, son and holy spirit. Now I'm more of a set-me-on-fire-and-scatter-me-to-the-wind kind of gal, but maybe this wouldn't be a bad place to spend eternity.

I was surprised to find that each grave, regardless of age, was immaculately kept. Some had shiny marble stones, polished brass nameplates and pots of fresh flowers, while others had nothing to show but time.

All that's clear enough to read on this one is *Cher Ange* or dear angel, whose angel remains a mystery. I think back to all the people who died in my presence, someone's parent or child, a sibling, a friend, a lover, and I wonder what became of the departed. Ascension to paradise, dust to dust, descent to the fiery depths, reincarnated accordingly? Who knows? All I know is that no one gets out alive so I'd better get busy.

I figure I'll hedge my bets. If to dust I shall return then I've got some hell raising to do. If there's a heaven then I've got a Bible to buy and some praying to do. If reincarnation is in my future then I've got a lot of work left ahead of me to move up from a future as a sewer rat. Wherever I end up, I hope there's a cellar full of French wine and a man named Neil holding two glasses and a corkscrew.

TAKE TWO ASPIRIN
AND CALL ME IN A YEAR

I used to tell my patients that nothing in this life is a waste of time as long as we learn from it (people actually paid me for this). From the calendar I see that my 365th day in France is fast approaching and it's time for this psychiatrist to swallow her own medicine and review the lessons learned from 12 months of wasted time.

While I've spent more than half my life being taught everything from algebra to the neurochemistry of schizophrenia, my year of nothing has probably been the most educational one of my life. First, and by now this should come as no surprise, I've learned that I'm not very good with languages. But I have a newfound ability to be optimistic in the face of persistent failure. I also choose to see constant corrections by strangers as kindness, a trait the French people I've met have in abundance. I speak and understand far more than when I first arrived, so I'm giving myself a shiny gold star on that one.

I've also discovered that it takes time for an obsessive overachiever to change her ways. I came looking to simplify my life yet within a month of arriving of I was fully entangled in yet another real estate drama. Now, from my perfectly imperfect housette, I see my many renovations for what they really were, an endless striving for perfection. House, career, car, thighs, it doesn't matter. It was all a silly race with no possible finish line. And while I can't take full credit for things working out as they did, I am proud of myself for finally accepting (and loving) a home just the way it is. If I can master "leave well enough alone" by the time I leave this world, I'll be a happy woman.

So what about happy? After all my years of therapy, both giving and receiving, I'm still not sure what that word actually means. People define happiness as it suits them and far be it for me to advise anyone how to achieve it. Certainly to the casual observer my former life had all the necessary elements for happiness. And in all honesty, I wasn't unhappy. I just felt out of place in my own life and I needed to find where I belonged. I'm still working on where I fit exactly, but I do know that my happiness has nothing to do with being called Doctor or the salary that goes with it. In fact, despite my recent whining about what I'm missing, going without has been one of my favourite lessons of all. Of course, there are still times when I feel I may actually die without a black wool trench coat, but then I remember something: I have everything I need.

Long before coming to France I gave some serious thought to leaving medicine in search of a new career. I even hired a consultant to help me understand what my options were. She stumped me with one question: "What would you like to do?" The trouble was I didn't have the foggiest idea. I realized that apart from reading, what I liked to do most was to go on vacation. I had no designs on becoming a ski instructor in Switzerland but when escaping your life becomes your major motivation, changes must be made. I considered going back to school but I was worn out, and the idea of four more years in classrooms was extremely unappealing. Then along came the opportunity here. Yes, it was still all about houses but at least they were other people's houses and I thought it was a step in the right direction. As for how that turned out, I've learned that no matter how hard I try to control my life, *merde* happens. On the surface of things it looks like the lesson here is the tried and true (or perhaps very tired and unlikely to be true) "things happen for a reason." But I see something more.

If I had to narrow it all down into one piece of wisdom it would be this: sometimes you have to step away from the many things you have to do to find the one thing you want to do. What began as a personal diary and a convenient way to keep friends and family updated has grown into an all out passion. Before starting a blog about my detour to France, all I'd ever written were prescriptions. Over the past year I've written something almost every day and while I have to be careful not to apply my Type A ways to it, writing brings me a pleasure I never dreamed possible. For now it doesn't matter if I'm any good at it, all that matters is that I feel good doing it.

Some will say that my story is nothing more than a grand exercise in self-absorption, that my year in France was a protracted and somewhat empty sabbatical, and they'd be right. Well, so what? From where I sit my time has been well squandered. I'm still reflecting on my choices (past and future) but I'm not so caught up in my own head to suggest that my way of learning things is practical for everyone. It's not, and my lessons are my own. But here's something I've always known: everything we need and desire can be found anywhere we choose to look for it. I chose to look in France and found myself. Of course, ditching your life and roaming halfway around the world just to find yourself is simply the method used by a responsible and level-headed psychiatrist. I'm sure there are more daring ways to go about it.

FRIENDS WITH BENEFITS

When I lived in Canada, I certainly had more friends to see but it seems that I actually see friends more in *ma vie française*. No wonder, with the old job and everything I had to give to it, I had very little left over for my social scene. Now, time is what I have the most of and I'm lucky to be able to spend it with new friends who offer me a different view of the world and of myself. Not for a moment am I suggesting that my Canadian friends offered me less than *mes amis* here. There's simply no measure of the love, laughter, wisdom and bail money that my buddies across the water have given and still give me. We often had a lot in common, our language, lifestyle and experiences. Here, it's a whole new game.

Take Geraldine, a woman I met at the country cookout awhile back and happened to run into again at *Mademoiselle* Elodie's torture chamber. Geraldine has a rickety knee to match my rickety spine but that's where the similarities end. She graciously invited us to her home a few miles away to share a meal and get to know each other a little more. She shares her life with Michel, her *mari* of 42 years, at the end of a country road.

We pulled up in the dwindling sunshine of the day and took a tour of their vast property, a stone farmhouse surrounded by rolling green hills as far as the eye can see. But never mind the scenery, she could be running her own grocery store from her garden. Every vegetable imaginable is raised by hand and brought to her table. She has fruit trees so laden with peaches, plums, pears and apples that the branches touch the ground. I thought poor Neil, a man who eats whole pies in one sitting, was going to have some sort of fruit fetish episode.

We went inside their beautiful home, which they themselves restored from top to bottom, and she served us a meal that has reinforced my belief that eating must be considered a religion. She's raised three children, manages a vacation cottage on her property, speaks French, English, Italian and Spanish, has sailed around the Mediterranean several times and has travelled the world. She has her hair cut in every foreign country she visits just to see how they do it (for the record, she loves her grey hair), and when she visited my house for dinner she brought me, as is the custom in France, these …

Two things to note here: the very classy, cut-off plastic water bottle we call a vase, and the fact that these flowers are from her garden. So wife, mother, linguist, chef, interior designer, farmer, sailor, world explorer, tourism entrepreneur and, apparently, florist. I've only spent two evenings with her so far and god only knows what'll come out next. If she told me she was running Spain from her garage I'd believe her. All this begs one question and one question only: what have I been doing with my time? Granted, she's got a few years on me, but still. She's a talented and brilliant woman with fascinating stories. But more importantly, she's engaging, unassuming and incredibly gracious. She's an inspiration, and in many ways, represents the sort of woman I've always wanted to be.

A year ago, I never would've believed that such a life actually existed. Now, seeing it up close, I'm determined to figure out how to make every minute of mine count, to make a life that I can look back on and be well pleased. Okay, maybe not the cooking (I already have a husband) or the four languages (don't get me started), and as for the sailing, I get seasick just looking at boats. But little by little I'll find my way. Maybe I'll start with the raising three kids thing. How hard could it be?

A LIFE LESS EXTRAORDINARY

It's the 16th of September and for the better part of my adult life I've been waiting for this day. No matter what happens tomorrow, from this day on, I can say I once lived in France for a year. And what a strange and glorious year it's been. So many times I've asked myself what was I thinking. Well, looking back on how it came to be, I do remember two certainties I held before turning my life upside down, and today seems like the perfect time to see just how right or wrong I was.

The first was that I love my husband. While I was sure of it the day I married him, even more so in the moment of decision to leave everything, what I'm unsure of now is how to describe what I feel for him after this last year together. Here's a man who arrived in a foreign country and created an entire life from absolutely nothing. He's done all the talking, officially speaking, a *soupçon* of irony there, one thinks. He's opened bank accounts, met with French accountants, researched international tax laws and incorporated his business here … I made a banana bread. He then turned to matters of domestic policy. He secured a residency permit, bought and unbought a house, negotiated a complicated lease, set up utility contracts and is in the process of acquiring state health care for us. All while working full-time and receiving orders for buckets of *boeuf bourguignon* from some woman who occasionally does a bit of laundry for him.

Of course, those who record history can take credit for events as they see fit. So it's tempting for me as the scribe of our life to depict myself as some adventurous heroine bravely forging a new life in France. But the truth is this might be the only time in history when a great man has triumphed without the help of an even greater woman. I think he's a genius and the most generous person I've ever known. And now, this year has given him a shine that threatens to burn the eyes right out of my head. He made it all by himself without a single complaint, then handed it to me, asking nothing in return. No words can describe receiving it but I do have a new certainty: love is too weak a word.

The second thing I was sure of was that I needed to transform my life into something unrecognizable from the one I'd been living; that my daily grind was grinding me straight into the ground. I was so busy looking closely into the lives of others that I had no time for even a passing glance at my own. Granted, I didn't have to pack up and move to France, desperate times and all that, but I did have to leave my job. I'm well aware that I'm a tad daffy these days but I used to be a very serious psychiatrist, a soldier eye deep in the trenches of the mental health care system. The post I retired from was on a locked child and adolescent psychiatric unit forgotten by the public and government funding; an incredibly busy place where unspeakable and, for me unwriteable, tragedies were revealed on a daily basis. Only now with distance do I fully feel the impact of the horrors those kids survived and, on the really bad days, did not survive.

More than once over the last year I've had doubts and fears about what will become of me job wise and I've second (and third and fourth) guessed the wisdom of leaving a career I worked so hard to have. I mean who in their right mind spends fifteen years in school and over a hundred grand for a career, only to leave at its peak? But while I was at Madame Geraldine's place the other night, something happened that set this old brain of mine at ease.

We were chatting at the table after a marvelous dinner when in walked a couple with a child about seven or eight years old. They were friends of the family passing through the area and bedding down at the farmhouse for the night. I started to introduce myself when I noticed the child was suddenly right at my side. He waited for me to stop talking and then without a word he smiled, leaned in and placed a soft and slightly sticky kiss on my right cheek, then another on my left. He walked silently to Neil, did the same then skipped up the stairs to bed. In that moment of sweetness from a seemingly happy child who had no terrible secret to tell, no wounds to be healed, I felt a freedom from my old worries and responsibilities that I need to keep.

Every person who has ever called me Doctor got my very best but I knew then and there I wouldn't go back. Later that night, I thought about all the kids I've cared for who inspired this journey in the first place. I recall being in their company and finding myself quite ordinary. Not much has changed on that front. Sure, I live an unusual life in an out of the ordinary place, but I don't think I'll ever come close to discovering the secret of their grace. Instead of the extraordinary life I was seeking, I found one more ordinary than ever before. But somehow I think they'd approve of what I've done and that's good enough for me.

I walked away from a solid career and now I have no idea what's next for me—scary indeed. I came here with a plan for work that dissolved away into the nothingness of the life I now live, scarier still. But these days I find myself less concerned with the things that used to consume me. Actually, I find myself, well, just less concerned. So as I see it, at least for today, I walked toward something infinitely more valuable. Say what you will about the cliché of a midlife crisis, I highly recommend it. Maybe what I've done will inspire someone else to look at their life a little more closely, maybe not. Maybe this next year will be a perfect example of what not to do with your life, who knows? I sure as hell don't. Here's what I do know: *je ne regrette rien.*

To those who thought me impulsive and foolish to run away from the circus, you may be right. When I started all this I said I'd lost my mind and that may also be true. But today, walking through this town I now call home, I found something better. As I slowly made my way over the ancient Pont Pinard and began the climb to my housette, I was overcome with a strange warmth, a bizarre sensation that I couldn't quite put my finger on. At first I thought I was having my first hot flash or some sort of stroke. So I stopped walking, closed my eyes and then it came to me. It was joy. Who knew I had it in me? Now if I could just find some sour cream.

Acknowledgments

Saying thank you is one of my favourite things to do. So first and foremost, *merci beaucoup* to all the fine people of Semur-en-Auxois especially *Monsieur le Maire* Philippe Guyenot and the staff at *la Mairie*, *Monsieur* Francis Gally and *Les Gueux*, *Monsieur* Eric Moreau, *Monsieur* Patrick Dano, *Monsieur* Sébastien Morvan, *Monsieur* Serge Bierry, *Café Des Arts*, *Galerie Spiralinthe*, *Hotel Chassy* and *Le Chœur des Ambrosiniens*. I hope the *Semurois* feel their town has been given the respect it deserves.

My heartfelt thanks to Donna Francis, Pam Dooley and everyone at Creative Book Publishing for taking a chance on a very new and clueless writer who I am sure nearly drove them right round the bloody bend, for allowing me the opportunity to tell my stories the way I wanted to tell them and for making my first foray into publishing a happy one.

To Jill Hatchette, Michel Devrient, Mary Tod and especially Damhnait Monaghan, thank you for suffering through the first draft and for your gentle and helpful counsel. I also want to express my profound gratitude to Vivian Swift for her uncommonly generous guidance, support and enthusiasm.

My stories are true and come from real people whose kindness knows no limits. Michel, Patricia, Gaëtan and Florian, Anne and Michel, Elizabeth, Patricia, Francis, Jacqueline, Ulysse and Eleanor, Geraldine and Michel, Steve, Jean-Claude and Jacqueline, Elodie, *merci bien*. And to my family and friends, thank you for being so incredibly supportive of this journey and for not once saying (to my face at least) that I was silly to do this.

We live in the age of social media and, good or evil, this book would not exist without it. Tara Bradbury (*merci Madame*), a reporter who happened to appear on my Twitter account one day, introduced me to my publisher, so really it's all her fault. And on a Friday night way back when, I emailed my brother-in-law and technical genius Scott to say that I was thinking of starting a blog. By Monday morning it was up and running. I still have no idea how my own website works but he does, and for that and many other things, I thank him. To my blog followers, affectionately known as the Finders, no words could possibly express my gratitude (a special *merci* to Betsy Lerner for introducing me to many of them). Their relentless encouragement has seen me through this adventure and hopefully they'll be with me for whatever comes next. They are without a doubt the most wonderful people I've never met.

Finally, I'd like to say that marriage is a team sport. So I thank my photographer Neil McCulloch. While some of the pictures in this book are mine, if it's a great one then it's his. I also offer him my thanks for designing this book, including the beautiful cover. As for everything else he's done for me, I'll say no more. I'm not about to portray him as a saint any more than I already have. Next thing he'll think he's got the upper hand and ask me to cook something or take out the garbage. Not a chance buddy.